Ultralight Flight

by Michael A. Markowski

The Pilot's Handbook Of Ultralight Knowledge

Ultralight Flight —
The Pilot's Handbook of Ultralight Knowledge
by Michael A. Markowski

Copyright © 1982 by Michael A. Markowski

FIRST EDITION
First Printing - November 1982

Published by:
Ultralight Publications
Post Office Box 234
Hummelstown, PA 17036

All rights reserved, including the right to reproduce this book or portions thereof in any form or by any means, electronic or mechanical, including photocopying, recording, or by an information storage or retrieval system without written permission from the author, except for the inclusion of brief quotations in a review. All rights are also reserved for translation into foreign languages. No liability is assumed with respect to use of the information herein, nor is endorsement of any product implied or intended.

Books by the Author
THE HANG GLIDER'S BIBLE, The Complete Pilot's and Builder's Guide.
THE ENCYCLOPEDIA OF HOMEBUILT AIRCRAFT, including Powered Hang Gliders.
ULTRALIGHT AIRCRAFT, The Basic Handbook of Ultralight Aviation
ULTRALIGHT FLIGHT, The Pilot's Handbook of Ultralight Knowledge

Library of Congress Cataloging in Publication Data

Markowski, Michael A., 1947 —
Ultralight Flight, The Pilot's Handbook of Ultralight Knowledge
(Ultralight Aviation Series, No. 3)
Bibliography: p.
  1. Ultralight aircraft. 2. Ultralight aircraft — Handling characteristics.
I. Title. II. Series.
TL761.M33 1982   629.1'4   81-71889
ISBN 0-938716-07-7
ISBN 0-938716-06-9 (pbk.)

On The Cover

The "Hawk" leads the way toward a new era in ultralight flight. It features conventional stick, rudder and flap controls, and is powered by the 30 hp Cuyuna 430-R. Courtesy CGS Aviation, Inc.

Dedication

In memory of my grandfather Matthew Sasa, who instilled in me the fascination of flight, with the gift of a rubber powered model airplane at age 5.

WARNING — A WORD OF CAUTION

Flight, in and of itself, is not necessarily dangerous, however it is most unforgiving of errors, sloppiness and misjudgment on the part of both the designer and pilot. Whenever a man flys, he accepts the risk that he may be injured or even killed. It is each individual's decision to either accept or reject this risk in light of its potential hazards, challenges and rewards. Flying can be and is done safely every day of the year by paying strict attention to the details.

This book is not intended as a do-it-yourself guide, but merely as a source of information to be used as a reference. If there is anything you don't understand, don't hesitate to ask your flight instructor. It is further recommended that you obtain a student pilot solo license and ground school before you attempt flight on your own. Ultralights are real airplanes, not toys, and they must be treated with respect.

About the Author

Mike Markowski's life literally revolves around flight. He is a graduate aeronautical engineer (specialized in low speed aerodynamics) and FAA licensed private pilot who, since 1971 has devoted his life to the development of ultralight aviation. He was instrumental in initiating hang gliding in the eastern regions of the United States, and began his writing career as editor of the original *Skysurfer* magazine. Prior to that, he was employed as an advanced research engineer for Douglas and Sikorsky aircraft companies, working in the areas of advanced designs and new concepts. Since then, he has built and flown many ultralights of his own design, founded two manufacturing firms, ran a flight school, taught ultralight flight theory at the university level (M.I.T. and others), and is considered an authority on ultralight aviation.

He has lectured to numerous organizations and groups, including the International Symposium on the Technology and Science of Low Speed and Motorless Flight held at M.I.T. He was also responsible for the Forum on Foot-Launched Flight held at the Annual Convention and Fly-In of the Experimental Aircraft Association during the mid-seventies. He has made "star" appearances on national television shows, is sought after for speaking engagements by various groups, and he is often quoted in books, magazines, and newspapers around the world.

Mike is a widely read author, having four books (The Hang Glider's Bible, The Encyclopedia of Homebuilt Aircraft, Ultralight Aircraft and Ultralight Flight) to his credit—classics in their fields—as well as numerous magazine articles.

In addition to writing and flying, Mike is an aeronautical consultant to the ultralight industry for engineering design, as well as marketing and advertising. He is also listed as the nation's only Technical Expert in Ultralight Aviation by Attorneys in the Products Liability and Transportation Legal Directory and, as such, is active in legal cases. He holds memberships in the Experimental Aircraft Association, Soaring Society of America, United States Hang Gliding Association, and the National Association of Sport Aircraft Designers.

It is hoped that this book will foster safety through education as ultralight aviation develops and grows into recreational flying of the future.

Contents

Introduction

Ever since the Wright Brothers successfully tested their "flyer" on the wind swept sands of Kitty Hawk, aeronautical engineers have been trying to design a flying machine the average working man could afford to own and keep at home. The world famous Piper "Cub" of the late 1940's is one well-known attempt, but it just didn't happen in the anticipated numbers — all the proper factors simply were not present. Today however, the situation is entirely different. The development of both the hang glider and snowmobile engine during the 1960's set the stage for a new form of aviation — in what appears to be an uncanny case of history repeating itself, but on a lighter weight, higher technological scale. The inevitable marriage between the technologies produced what are today known as ultralight aircraft.

Aside from being quite low in cost, the most significant thing about ultralights is that they need not be registered with the FAA, nor is the operator required to have a pilot's license. Granted, these aircraft won't set any new speed records, but neither will they cost a fortune to own and operate. A top-of-the-line model costs but one-fifth the price of a stripped-down basic light plane, and consumes as little as one gallon of regular auto gasoline an hour.

For the first time in history, an aircraft has been developed purely for recreational purposes, and is succeeding in that role. Until now, flying machines have always had to justify their existence either through military employment or by serving the needs of commerce and industry. With the ultralight, recreation is first; however, they can pay their own way too. Cattle ranchers and farmers are using them to survey the "south forty" and inspect the herd. With their inherent STOL (short takeoff and landing) capability, ultralights are a natural for this type of use. Landing rolls of 100 feet or less are typical. Advertising agencies are using them as large area, low and slow flying, aerial billboards. Ultralights are also being used by sportsmen for access to and from remote and otherwise inaccessible areas. Aerial photographers are finding ultralights quite handy while cutting operational expenses to almost nil. Pipeline surveys report similar experiences. Some agriculturalists are also experimenting with crop dusting applications, while a few enthusiasts even fly back and forth to work.

While most ultralights are flown under power, many can glide and soar under the proper conditions, and give an exhilaration that can't be duplicated in any other type of aircraft. They can be soared for hours in the updrafts formed on the windward side of a mountain, as well as climbing in thermals generated by the sun's heating of the earth's surface.

Flying an ultralight is truly flying. The pilot is not encased in a plexiglass and aluminum shell – he's not insulated from his atmospheric environment. Ultralights are on a scale that the average person can relate to. Instead of feeling like an intruder to the air, an ultralight allows you to touch the wind and become a part of the air. After the day's flying is over, the craft is folded-up and stored in the garage.

The "invention" of the ultralight airplane has its roots at the beginnings of aeronautical science. Like so many other man-made devices, it had to go through several stages before it was accepted to the point where it could become a viable, successful machine. The proper combination of technologies, in addition to such factors as world economy and a desire to simplify flying, has at last lead to the emergence of everybody's airplane.

A Special Acknowledgement

My sincerest thanks go out to Luis Marden of the National Geographic Society, for performing the formidable tasks of proof reading and copy editing. I deeply appreciate what you have done, and believe your efforts have made this a far better book than it otherwise would have been. I am certain my readers will benefit comenserately.

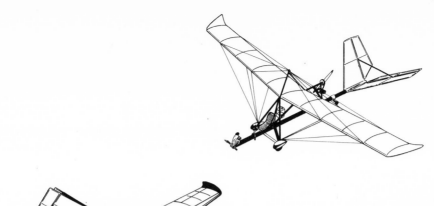

Section One
ULTRALIGHT
FOUNDATIONS

Chapter One

The Ultralight Vocabulary

Aerodynamics is the science that deals with the relative motion of objects through the air and the interactions developed therein. It is central to anything that flies. As theories have evolved over the years, terms have been developed to describe various phenomena. We will explain the more important terms to make the text more meaningful.

aerobatic   FAR (Federal Aviation Regulations) 91.71 defines aerobatic flight as an intentional maneuver involving an abrupt change in an aircraft's altitude, and abnormal attitude or abnormal acceleration not necessary for normal flight. Aerobatics are characterized by maneuvers such as loops, rolls, spins and inverted flight. An aircraft must be able to withstand ultimate load factors of +9.0 and -4.5 to be considered aerobatic. Ultralights are generally not designed for aerobatic flight.

aerodynamic center   The point on an airfoil where the pitching moment coefficient is constant from zero lift up to near the stall. It is usually located one quarter of the chord length behind the leading edge, and the lift and drag are assumed to act through it.

aerodynamic coefficient   A non-dimensional number which is the ratio of an aerodynamic force or moment, divided by the dynamic pressure and the wing area (and chord for moments), principally the coefficients of lift, drag, and pitching moment.

aerodynamic damping The aerodynamic forces that resist rotations about an aircraft's axes, and those that reduce rotations after a gust or control input is made.

aerodynamic force The force generated by a body's motion through the air.

aileron Plain flap control surfaces located at a wing's outer trailing edge. They deflect asymmetrically to rotate an aircraft about its longitudinal axis.

air A mechanical, not chemical, mixture of gases that comprise the earth's atmosphere. The main components are oxygen (78%) and nitrogen (21%) the rest being made up of several inert gases. The exact content of the mixture varies with altitude and latitude.

aircraft Any and all structures that are supported in the air either by its dynamic reaction with the air or by a buoyant gas. More specifically, the term applies to free and tethered balloons, blimps, dirigibles, kites, ornithopters, flying model airplanes, hang gliders, ultralights and other fixed wing aircraft, helicopters and autogyros.

airflow The movement of air. Its flow is measured as a mass of volume per unit time.

airfoil Any structure designed to gain a useful reaction from the airflow around it. More specifically, the cross sectional shape of a wing, tail surface, or propeller.

airframe The structural and aerodynamic components that support the loads transmitted to it by the parts in contact with the air. They include: fuselage, wings, tails, landing gear, tail booms, fairings, nacelles, and control surfaces.

airplane Any engine powered, heavier-than-air, fixed wing aircraft that generates lift solely by the dynamic reaction of the air with its surfaces.

airscoop The open end of a duct, hood, cowl or nacelle that projects into the airflow to carry a portion of that airflow to another part of the aircraft, such as an engine cooling air intake.

airspace The air above a certain area on the earth, typically identified by some sort of boundary.

airspeed The speed with which an aircraft moves relative to the air.

airstream The airflow.

airworthy When an aircraft is suitable for safe flight.

altitude The vertical distance of an aircraft above the surface. Altimeters are usually set with sea level being zero, and all navigational charts are zeroed to sea level.

amphibian An aircraft capable of operating off land and water.

angle of attack The angle a wing chord line makes with respect to the relative wind.

angle of climb The angle between the local horizon and the climb path of an aircraft.

angle of incidence The angle the wing chord line is set with respect to an airplane's longitudinal axis.

aspect ratio The slenderness of a wing defined as wingspan squared divided by wing area. Wingspan divided by average chord also yields aspect ratio.

atmospere The gaseous envelope surrounding the earth through which flight occurs. It extends up to about 700 miles above the surface, thinning out with altitude.

attitude The orientation of an aircraft's axes with respect to the horizon.

aviation The art and science of manned flight, especially with heavier-than-air vehicles.

axes Three imaginary straight lines that pass perpendicularly through an aircraft's center of gravity, around which the aircraft rotates. The axes include: vertical (yaw axis), longitudinal (roll axis), and lateral (pitch axis).

balloon The momentary, inadvertent rise of an airplane as it tries to touch down for a landing. It is normally caused by the pilot over-controlling the landing, and can be amplified by ground effect.

bank The tilt of an aircraft about its longitudinal axis, which is necessary to turn.

Bernoulli's Principle This most fundamentally important aspect of low speed aerodynamics was discovered in 1738 by a Swiss physicist named Daniel Bernoulli. He found that in any given airflow, the sum of the static and dynamic pressures was always the same, everywhere in the flow. What this means is that for any streamline flow wherever the velocity is high the pressure is lowered and, wherever the velocity is lowered the pressure is raised. For example, the air striking the leading edge of a wing is stopped at the stagnation point, resulting in a higher pressure. Also, whenever an airflow meets with a restriction, as in a venturi, the velocity must increase to move the same volume of air.

biplane An airplane with two sets of wings, one set above the other.

boundary layer The thin layer of air immediately adjacent to a surface over which air flows, composed of decelerated velocity air—the slowest air being nearest the surface. The boundary layer can be laminar—where the velocity deceleration is gradual, or turbulent—where the various velocities mix with one another.

burble The airflow condition above and behind a stalled wing. Turbulence.

camber The depth of an airfoil's mean line, expressed as a percentage of the chord.

canard Aircraft with a small lifting wing located ahead of the main wing. The small lifting wing itself.

ceiling, absolute The highest altitude attainable by an aircraft.

ceiling, service The altitude where the maximum rate of climb is 100 feet per minute.

center of gravity The point where an aircraft balances and, through which the force of gravity is considered to act. It is also the point where the three axes meet perpendicular to one another, and around which all motions are considered to occur.

center of pressure The point on a surface where the resultant of all the aerodynamic forces can be considered to act.

centripetal force The acceleration on a turning aircraft that causes it to turn. Specifically, it is the inward tilt of the wing's lift vector which counteracts the centrifugal force tending to prevent the aircraft from turning.

chord The length of an airfoil or wing section, as measured from leading edge to trailing edge.

circulation The motion of air rotating about an axis. Specifically, the air rotating about a lifting airfoil as a theory of lift.

Coanda effect The tendency of an airstream to attach itself to and follow the surface over which it flows. The surface should be smooth and rounded.

control surface Aerodynamic surfaces that move to control the altitude, speed and direction of an aircraft. These include: elevator, ailerons, rudders, flaps, spoilers, trim tabs and drag brakes.

crab Technique used to maintain course in a crosswind. It is established by a turn done in the normal way with aileron, while rudder is used to correct any adverse yaw. The aircraft will appear to be travelling sideways with respect to the ground but, it will be going straight with respect to the wind. Controls are then neutralized.

cruise speed The speed, below top speed, at which an aircraft normally flies for reasons of fuel economy and engine life. It generally occurs at throttle settings of 65% to 75% of wide open throttle.

delta wing Triangularly shaped wing with swept back leading edges and a straight trailing edge.

dihedral Small angle made between the horizontal and the wing panel chord plane.

downwash The downward flow of air behind a lifting wing.

drag The total aerodynamic force tending to retard the motion of an aircraft in a direction parallel to the airflow.

dynamic pressure The pressure developed when air comes to rest at the front of an object. It is measured in pounds per square foot and is often referred to as "q," which is the product of one-half the air density times the velocity squared.

dynamic stability The oscillating motion an aircraft exhibits in returning to its original flight trim condition.

eddy A small rotational turbulence within an airflow.

elevator The aft hinged portion of the horizontal stabilizer, or canard, which controls pitch attitude and airspeed.

elevon Dual purpose control surface on flying wings, used for both pitch and roll control.

empennage The horizontal and vertical tail group.

empty weight The weight of an aircraft unloaded and unoccupied, including: usable fuel, undrainable oil, engine coolant, hydraulic fluid and attached ballast weights.

engine cowling A fairing positioned around the engine, designed to direct cooling air through the engine in an aerodynamically efficient manner.

equilibrium A condition of balance. An aircraft is in equilibrium when lift equals weight and thrust equals drag.

fairing A streamlined shell placed over a structure or component to reduce drag.

fin The fixed leading portion of the vertical tail.

fineness ratio A body's length divided by its thickness. Optimal fineness ratios develop minimal drag for a given thickness.

fixed-pitch propeller A propeller with blades that are unadjustable in flight, as is typical for ultralights.

fixed-wing aircraft An airplane with a stationary wing and not a helicopter or rotary winged aircraft.

flap The hinged, moveable inboard trailing edge portion of a wing used to alter camber, and therefore lift and drag, especially during landing.

flight Movement of an aircraft through the atmosphere.

flutter A harmonic oscillation or vibration of an aircraft part or control surface caused by aerodynamic forces acting on a too flexible or improperly balanced component.

fluid Any liquid or gas.

flying wing An aircraft that houses all essentials for flight within the wing. It does not have a horizontal tail.

flying wires Cables located beneath the wing that support it against positive flight loads.

free stream The airflow outside the region affected by the passage of an aircraft.

fuselage The part of the airframe that houses the pilot, with wings, tail and landing gear attached to it.

g The acceleration subjected to an airplane by gravity and abrupt maneuvers. One g is generated in straight and level flight, due to the acceleration of gravity, which is 32 feet per second per second, acting on the mass of the aircraft.

gas The fluids that expand indefinitely, having no definite shape or volume.

glide Flight with little or no thrust, characterized by a loss in altitude.

glider An engineless aircraft that derives its thrust from gravity.

glide ratio Numerically equal to the lift over drag (L/D) ratio, it is the horizontal distance an aircraft will travel (engine-off) for every foot of altitude lost.

gross weight An aircraft's total flying weight, including: empty weight, fuel, oil, pilot, passengers and cargo.

ground effect The tendency for an aircraft to "float" when within a half wingspan of the runway. It's caused by a reduction in induced drag.

hang glider Engineless aircraft from which the pilot is suspended in a harness or swing seat. It is typically controlled by weight shifting, but may incorporate aerodynamic controls as well. They are normally footlaunched and landed.

induced drag That portion of the drag due to the generation of lift. It is associated with wing tip vortices and is most important at low speeds.

joystick The control stick. It is connected to ailerons and elevator on three axis controlled aircraft and, to rudder and elevator on two control aircraft.

kilo One kilogram, which equals about 2.2 pounds.

kinetic energy The energy possessed by a body due to its motion.

kite Generally, an aircraft flown while tethered to the ground or a ground based vehicle. It flys solely by the relative wind pressure against its surfaces. Also, colloquilly, a Rogallo-type hang glider.

laminar flow Airflow characterized by streamlines that move smoothly over one another, without mixing.

landing gear The undercarriage on which an aircraft rests while on the ground. Typically wheels, it can be floats and skis, as well.

landing speed The airspeed with which an aircraft touches the ground, typically equal to the stall speed.

landing wires Cables located above the wing that support it against landing and negative flight loads.

lateral axis The imaginary line passing from wingtip to wingtip, through the center of gravity. Pitch motions occur about it.

lateral stability Stability about the roll axis.

leading edge The front of a wing.

lift The total aerodynamic force developed to support an aircraft perpendicular to the airstream.

lift coefficient The non-dimensional number which represents the lift of a wing or airfoil. It is obtained by dividing the lift by the free stream dynamic pressure and wing area.

limit load factor The number of g's an aircraft is designed to handle in flight.

load factor The total g load on an airplane from gravity and other accelerations.

longeron The primary longitudinal structural member of a fuselage.

longitudinal axis The imaginary line passing from nose to tail through the center of gravity. Rolling motions occur about it.

longitudinal stability Stability about the pitch axis.

maneuvering speed The highest allowable speed for abrupt maneuvers or very rough air. It is typically set at twice the stall speed and is designed to protect against structural failure. Here, the aircraft could receive a maximum 4 g load, where the wing would stall before loading the airframe further.

mean aerodynamic chord (MAC) The average chord of the wing, or wings, which can be used to represent an aircraft's center of aerodynamic forces.

mean line The center line of an airfoil section equidistant between the upper and lower surfaces.

minimum flying speed The lowest airspeed attainable, out of ground effect.

moment A force times its distance from the center of action (rotation).

momentum The quantity of motion, expressed as mass times velocity.

monocoque A type of fuselage construction in which the skin carries all or most of the stresses.

mush A nose high condition of flight between minimum power required speed and minimum level speed. It is flight on the "back side of the power curve."

navigation Act of directing flight from point to point.

negative g A condition that loads an aircraft from the top.

oscillation Vibration or movement to either side of a neutral point.

parasite drag Drag caused by components that do not contribute to lift. It becomes more important with speed.

parasol wing A monoplane with its wing strut mounted above the fuselage.

pitch A rotation about the lateral axis, as in nose-up, nose-down.

pitching moment The moment about an aircraft's lateral axis. A nose-up pitching moment is positive.

phugoid A long period longitudinal oscillation where an aircraft flies along a "roller-coaster" path with little or no change in angle of attack.

planform The top view of an object, particularly a wing.

power loading Pounds gross weight divided by horsepower.

potential energy The energy possessed by an object due to its height.

pressure altitude Height in the atmosphere as measured from the standard pressure datum of sea level.

profile The cross section of a body, especially the airfoil section of a wing.

propeller Airfoil shaped rotating wing used to convert torque into thrust. Larger diameters and lower tip speeds are more efficient.

propeller pitch The distance a prop moves forward for each revolution.

range Maximum distance an aircraft can fly at a given cruising speed, with a 45 minute reserve.

rate of climb Vertical speed of an aircraft. Typically quoted as a maximum at standard sea level conditions.

relative wind In the study of aerodynamics, it makes no difference whether an aircraft is flying through still air, or air is being blown past a stationary aircraft. The aerodynamic forces generated are identical.

Reynolds number The basic law of airflow similarity which is the ratio of dynamic forces divided by viscous forces. Airflow patterns are the same for similar Reynolds numbers.

rib The part of a wing that provides the airfoil shape.

Rogallo wing A flexible membrane sail-type wing as used on most hang gliders.

rudder Moveable part of vertical tail used to yaw aircraft. It balances adverse aileron yaw in independent three-axis control aircraft. Helps steer the aircraft while taxiing. It is NOT analogous to a ship's rudder and is not used like one!

ruddervator Dual purpose surface on V-tailed aircraft used to control pitch and yaw.

sailplane High performance glider with a glide ratio of 25 or better.

scale effect The affect of size on aerodynamic reactions. Generally, the larger an aerodynamic body, the more efficient it can be.

seaplane Aircraft designed for operations off water only.

separation When air fails to follow the contour of the object over which it is flowing. It occurs behind bluff bodies and more important, on the upper surface of wings at high angles of attack.

sink rate The vertical speed of descent, typically quoted as the minimum rate for the aircraft.

slat High lift device, located at the leading edge, that directs high velocity air over a wing to delay the stall.

slot The gap between a slat and a wing.

slope lift Wind striking vertical terrain generates this vertical wind on which gliders soar.

span Wing length from tip to tip.

spar A wing's primary load bearing member.

spin An aerobatic maneuver or a condition where an aircraft is stalled and rotating in a small radius about a vertical axis. The nose is pointed well below the horizon, as well.

spoiler Control surface located on wing's upper surface, which normally lies flush. When deflected, it reduces lift and increases drag. They roll the aircraft when deflected singly, and control glide path when deflected simultaneously.

square-cube law As a body is increased in size, its mass grows as the cube of its increase, while its area grows only as the square. In other words, doubling the linear dimension of an airplane will result in eight times the weight, and only four times the wing area, provided the construction and materials are similar. This also implies a doubling of the wing loading.

stagger On a biplane, the relative longitudinal spacing between leading edges. Positive stagger is when the top wing is forward, while negative stagger is when the bottom wing is forward.

stagnation point The forward location on a body where the airflow comes to rest, as on the leading edge of a wing section.

stall A breakdown in the lift of a wing which occurs when the airflow separates from the upper surface at an angle of attack peculiar to the airfoil section, Reynolds number and aspect ratio.

static pressure The ambient pressure of the atmosphere, normally 14.7 psi at sea level.

streamline The path traced by air molecules as they move over an object.

sweepback The angle the wing leading edge (or quarter chord line) makes with the lateral axis.

taildragger An aircraft with main wheels in front and a tail wheel, or skid.

thermal A parcel of heated air that breaks away from the ground and rises, usually generated over dark areas of the earth. Gliders use the updraft to gain altitude.

thrust The propelling force generated by a propeller, needed to overcome drag.

thrust line The imaginary centerline of the thrust, which is typically near or at the aircraft's center line.

tip dragger Wing tip control on some ultralights used to yaw the aircraft when actuated singly, and to control glide path when actuated simultaneously.

tip stall The stalling of a wing tip. It could occur at higher lift coefficients and develop into a spin. A properly designed wing should not tip stall—the stall should begin at the center of the wing.

trailing edge Aftermost portion of a wing.

tricycle landing gear Aircraft landing gear with a nose wheel and two main wheels aft the center of gravity. This is the most popular type, and it is stable.

turbulence The mixing of streamlines in an irregular "eddying" motion, such as is found behind bodies that have experienced a flow separation. Also, uneven movement of the atmosphere found mostly near the surface and behind obstructions. It can be strong enough to destroy an aircraft.

ultralight An aircraft with an empty weight under 254 pounds, a stall speed of 27 mph, and a top level speed of 63 mph, according to the FAA definition.

vector A force or speed that has both magnitude and direction. They can be added graphically by joining heads to tails or mathematically by trigonometry.

velocity never exceed (Vne) The red-line speed of an aircraft, beyond which structural damage may occur in calm air.

venturi A tube with a smaller diameter in the center than at the ends. When air, or any fluid, moves through a venturi, the velocity increases in the center, while the pressure decreases.

vertical axis Imaginary line which passes vertically through the aircraft's center of gravity and about which the aircraft yaws.

viscosity The "stickiness" of air as evidenced by its tendency to adhere to surfaces over which it flows, as well as to itself.

vortices Organized circular flow of air caused by pressure differences in an airflow. Examples include the "bound vortex" equivalent of a wing in circulation theory, and vortices developed at a wing tip.

washout Upward set of wing tip trailing edge to minimize tip stall.

weight and balance The practice of keeping an aircraft's gross weight and center of gravity within prescribed limits as established by the designer. Deviation from this results in poor performance and possibly catastrophic instability.

wind milling A propeller being turned by the airstream and not the engine.

wind tunnel Basically, a tube with a fan installed in one end to draw air over an object mounted inside the "test section." The object is connected to a sensitive balance system in order to measure aerodynamic forces and moments.

Chapter Two

The Ultra-Early Days

In his ages old quest for flight, man has conceived, built and flown all manner of devices to lift him from the clutches of Mother Earth. This chapter will show you some of the interesting minimum flying machines he has devised in his urge to defy gravity with simplicity.

In order to gain a better understanding of and appreciation for taday's ultralight, it is useful to go back in time to look at what has already been done. It is important to study history so that we can avoid repeating dangerous mistakes. Furthermore, in light of the scientific and technological advances that have since occurred, we may find it desirable to resurrect an old concept and refine it. An idea or configuration that was impractical only a few short years ago may be revolutionary today because of new methods, materials and techniques.

The powered ultralight airplane has been in existence since before the turn of the century! Several early aeronautical pioneers, in fact, had designs for ultralights which grew out of their hang gliding experiments—much as today's ultralight industry is an outgrowth of modern hang gliding. Had those pioneers survived, powered flight may well have come before the Wright's outstanding achievement.

The growth of modern ultralight aviation is one of the most remarkable events in the history of aviation. Discounting the famous "flight" of Icarus and Daedalus, as recorded in Greek mythology—as well as countless other unsuccessful birdmen

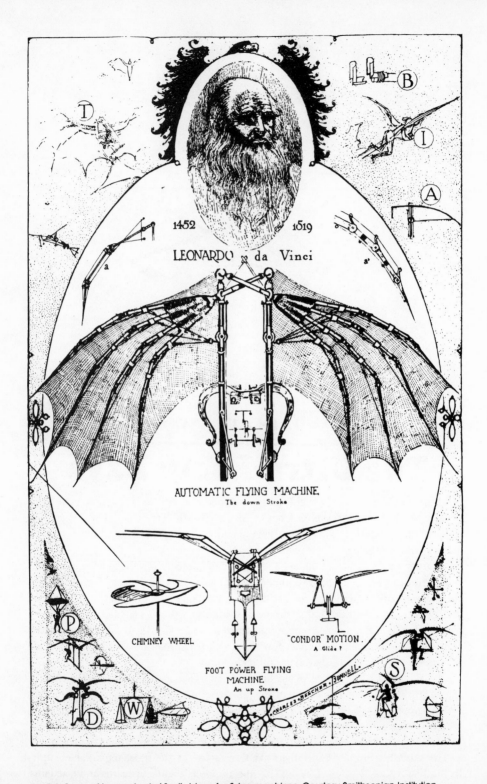

Fig. 2-1. Some of Leonardo da Vinci's ideas for flying machines. Courtesy Smithsonian Institution.

and tower jumpers, today's ultralight can trace its practical beginnings to the late nineteenth century with the daring hang gliding experiments of a few dedicated engineers. Furthermore, today's ultralight is a direct offspring or, shall we say, inspiration of the Rogallo flexible wing hang glider. It's a development that has been waiting for a lightweight "prime mover," and required a break from traditional aeronautical thinking before it would happen.

During the last two decades of the past century a few ingenious inventors not only had the nerve, but also the knowledge to design and construct practical flying machines. These men of vision saw hang gliding as the most exhilarating sport imaginable—they were way ahead of their time. Often ridiculed by the public, they practiced their art mostly in seclusion, for fear of public scorn.

Toward the very end of the 1890's, some scientists and engineers believed they had found the secret to the elusive ways of the bird—suddenly it became acceptable to invent flying machines.

Leonardo da Vinci

Often called the first modern, this fifteenth century artist, architect, engineer, and scientist devoted considerable observation, study and thought to the possibility of flight. He wrote in Codex Atlanticus: "A bird is an instrument working according to mathematical law, which instrument it is within the capacity of men to reproduce with all its movements, but not with a corresponding degree of strength, though it is deficient only in the power of maintaining equilibrium. We may therefore say that such an instrument constructed by man is lacking in nothing except the life of the bird, and this life must needs be supplied from that of man."

"The life which resides in the bird's member will, without doubt, better conform to their needs than will that of men which is separated from them, and especially in the almost imperceptible movements which preserve equilibrium. But since we see that the bird is equipped for many obvious varieties of movements, we are able from this experience to deduce that the most rudimentary of these movements will be capable of being comprehended by man's understanding; and that he will to a great extent be able to provide against the destruction of that instrument of which he has himself become the living principle and the propeller."

Da Vinci was intelligent enough to conclude that the flight of soaring birds required little actual effort, and deduced that man ought to be able to propel himself through the air. He went on to write: "A man, when flying, shall be free from the waist up, that he may be able to keep himself in equilibrium as he does in a boat, so that the center of gravity and of the instrument may be set itself in equilibrium and change when necessity requires it to the changing of the center of resistance."

There are rumors and statements to the effect that da Vinci actually flew, however it has not been proven so.

Sir George Cayley

Cayley, the Father of British aviation, built the first man-carrying aircraft in the early 1850's. His contributions to aviation cannot be overstated. In the words of M. Alphonse Breguet, a great French writer and student of aeronautics: "The name of Sir George Cayley must be placed in letters of gold at the beginning of the history of aviation."

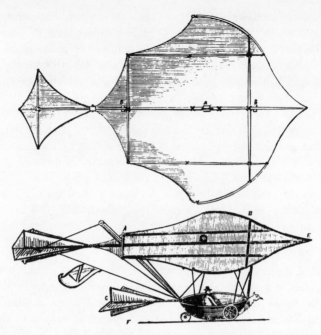

Fig. 2.2. Sir George Cayley's ultralight glider of the 1850's - the first man-carrying aircraft.

Sir George summarized the question of flight thus: "the whole problem is confined within those limits, i.e., to make a surface support a given weight by the application of power to the resistance of the air." Furthermore, he rightly favored the airplane over the dirigible as the logical choice for a flying machine, due to the handling difficulties caused by the great size of an airship.

It was Cayley who conceived the so-called "conventional" (tail behind the wing) configuration. He demonstrated wing incidence and how the tailplane could be set for automatic longitudinal stability, and tilted for pitch control. He also became aware of the dihedral angle and its contribution to lateral stability. Indeed, history records Cayley being responsible for manned flights of up to 1500 feet in the early 1850's, but no details of his glider were published. The best information available says his wings consisted of low aspect ratio sail-like surfaces stretched between leading and trailing edges. He also tried flapping wing experiments, but concluded man's strength as insufficient for flight.

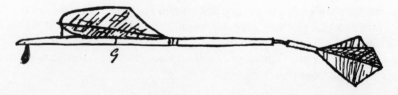

Fig. 2-3. Cayley was the first to conceive of the tail for automatic stability. This model glider dates to 1804.

F. H. Wenham

Wenham is important in consideration of his appreciation for high aspect ratio and the superposing of wings in a biplane or multiplane fashion. He took his que from nature in that soaring birds possess long slender wings and added the practical consideration of stacking surfaces for a more compact and stronger construction. In a paper presented in 1866 to the Royal Aeronautical Society's first men he wrote: "Having remarked how thin a structure is displaced beneath the wings of a bird in rapid flight, it follows that, in order to obtain the necessary length of plane for supporting heavy weights, the surfaces may be superposed, or placed in paralled rows, with an interval between them. A dozen pelicans may fly one above the other without material impediment, as if framed together, and it is thus shown him two hundred weight may be supported in a transverse distance of only ten feet."

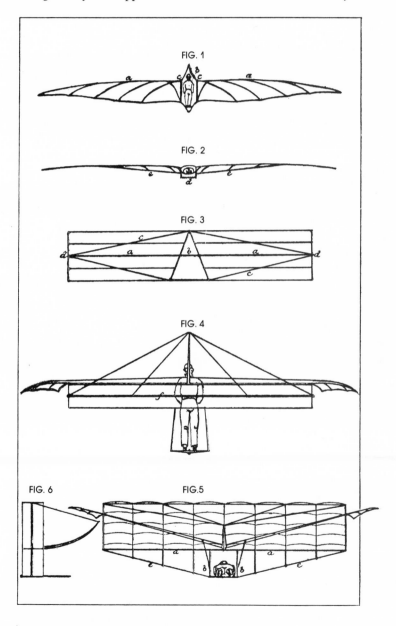

Fig. 2-4. F. H. Wenham used these drawings to illustrate his ideas of the value of multiplane construction in 1866.

Otto Lilienthal

Lilienthal was without question a most significant figure in the history of ultralight aviation. He was really the first person in history to have deliberately and audaciously sworn himself to become accustomed to the air. And being an experienced engineer, he was knowledgeable enough to apply his ideas to building and flying a true aircraft. His thinking was to first learn how to control the machine in flight before even considering the addition of power. Furthermore, he was intelligent enough to keep his gliders as simple as possible, (i.e., no flaps or other hinged surfaces) and rely on weight shift for control.

Lilienthal was also a gifted experimenter and writer. After many years of bird observation and before he flew, he published his classic book *Bird Flight as the Basis of Aviation,* establishing the foundations of modern day aerodynamics. His most profound conclusion was the superiority of curved wing sections over flat planes.

Otto actually began hang gliding in 1891 and eventually had a conical hill formed and a hangar built on top, so he could launch into any direction from which the wind was blowing. He built and successfully flew both biplanes and monoplanes until 1896, when he was planning to fit a 2½ HP carbonic motor to his latest glider. Power was to be transmitted to flapping wingtips, controlled by hand operated valves. Unfortunately, while practicing with a hang glider he crashed and was killed. As he lay dying, he uttered these immortal words: "Sacrifices must be made."

All told, Lilienthal made over 2000 glides and covered distances of up to a quarter mile in winds as high as 22 mph. He had proven, beyond the shadow of a doubt, that human flight was indeed possible and practical.

For the 1896 edition of the *Aeronautical Annual,* Otto predicted ultralight gliding quite correctly:

Fig. 2-5. Otto Lilienthal poses with his ultralight monoplane glider. Muse de l'Air.

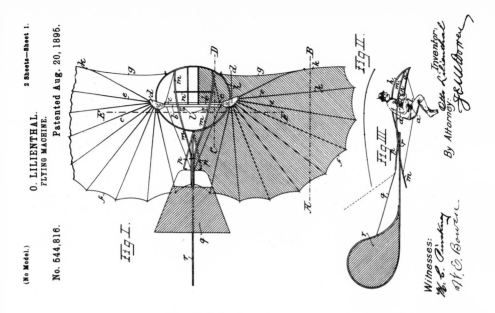

Fig. 2-6. Patent drawing for Lilienthal's "flying machine."

"Just as it is in sports in the water, so it is in sports in the air, that the greatest aim will be to reach the most startling results. The machines themselves, as well as the adroitness of their operator, will vie with each other.

He who succeeds in flying the fartherest from a certain starting point will come forth from the contest as conqueror. This fact will necessarily lead to the production of more and more improved flying apparatus. In a short time we shall have improvements of which today we have not the faintest idea.

The foundation for such a development exists already; it only needs a more thorough carrying out to gain perfection. The greater the number is of such persons who have the furthering of flying and the perfecting of the flying apparatus at heart the quicker we shall succeed in reaching a perfect flight. It is therefore of paramount importance that as many physically and technically well-trained men as possible take interest in these affairs, and that an apparatus be constructed which is as convenient and as inexpensive as possible."

Lawrence Hargrave

Working alone is Australia, this experimenter designed and flew model monoplanes and invented the box kite. His models were powered variously by rubber, compressed air, and steam engines which flapped wings or turned propellers for thrust. The ultimate development of his model work was the rotary engine configuration, aviation's most popular powerplant during WWI. Hargrave's box kites though, were his most important contribution to aeroscience, for they served as the basis for all biplanes to come. Indeed Hargrave himself boldly predicted in 1895 that, "in all probability it [Ed. the cellular kite] will prove to be the permanent type of the supporting surfaces of flying machines."

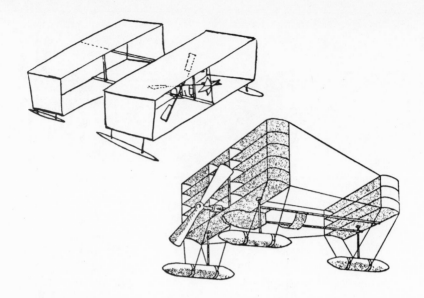

Fig. 2-7. Lawrence Hargraves' designs for man-carrying ultralights. Top is 1896 concept for a powered boxkite. Above is his 1902 multiplane of tinplate fitted with floats, but he lacked a suitable engine.

Octave Chanute

Chanute's importance in the evolution of ultralight aircraft is difficult to overstate. A well known and respected bridge builder and president of the Society of Civil Engineers, he also authored a great aeronautical classic called "Progress In Flying Machines" (1894). This monumental work chronicled over 400 years of flying experiments, mostly ultralight, including some of Lilienthal's highly successful work. The book, together with the man, formed a vital communicative

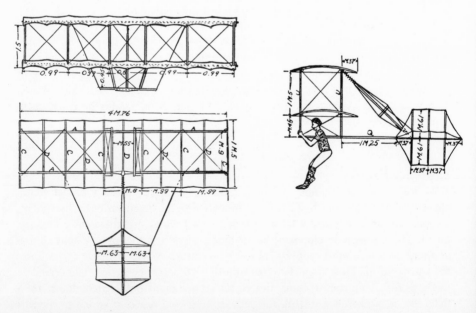

Fig. 2-8. Three-view drawing of the Chanute-Herring ultralight glider.

link in the then widely dispersed aeronautical world. Chanute also corresponded quite heavily with the Wright Brothers for some ten years before, during, and after their first flight. He served both as a source of information and confidant, as well as giving the brothers continuing encouragement.

Chanute's greatest contribution to ultralight design was probably the application of the Pratt truss, which had been patented in 1844, as a method of bracing railroad bridges. Using a biplane arrangement (originally advocated by Hargrave), and co-designed with mechanical engineer Augustus Herring, the two wings were connected by vertical posts braced by crisscrossing wires in both the longitudinal and lateral planes. This formed a rigid yet lightweight cellule structure that became the choice of the Wrights as well as all future biplane designs. The Chanute-Herring hang glider also incorporated Cayley's aft tail assembly for longitudinal stability, and a parabolic airfoil section for improved lift.

An article from "The Sunday Journal" of September, 1896 discusses Chanute's hang gliding experiments.

"The first experiment made was using the new machine as a "skimmer," that is, without motor or propeller, with the intention of literally studying the subject of "aspiration" (the ability to sail straight in the face of the wind without the slightest motion of its wings).

A run was made by experimenter William Avery along the side of a hill, he jumping into the air and governing the apparatus in the wind gusts. The first flight carried the operator fifty feet, he being at the time never less than two feet above the ground. This was considered an astounding result, considering that absolutely no motive power beyond the wind was used, and it demonstrated that the idea of

Fig. 2-9. Augustus Herring about to launch his biplane ultralight glider. Courtesy Smithsonian Institution.

the automatic regulator (a Herring devised spring-loaded articulated tail) was correct in principle.

After that first skim, Avery and Herring made between 150 and 200 jumps, all without the slighest accident, either to themselves or the machine. These jumps varied in length from 50 to 100 feet, and each one proved beyond question of doubt that the apparatus is perfectly manageable, automatically stable, strong enough in every part.

In confirming these early experiments to jumping with the machine, Mr. Chanute has followed the line which he has long advocated, "that the chief problem which is to be solved before man can hope to fly in the air is that of safety. He holds that this must first be worked out in a full-sized apparatus, mounted by a man and exposed to the vicissitudes of the wind, before any attempt is made to soar or apply a motor or propelling instrument."

Before long, Herring would leave Chanute and make some startling achievements on his own.

Percy Pilcher

England's greatest ultralight pioneer, Percy Pilcher, may well have been very close to a successful powered hang glider when he was tragically killed in a hang gliding accident. His much flown "Hawk" was going to be modified per detail engineering drawings, to accept a motor that was then being built. Pilcher had also designed and built a triplane that was put on public display on September 30, 1899 (the day of his fatal accident) at Rugby, England. It featured a horizontally opposed twin cylinder air cooled engine of 40 pounds, mounted at the nose. A long drive shaft ran over the pilot's head and connected to an aft mounted pusher

Fig. 2-10. Percy Pilcher and his "Hawk" ultralight glider. Courtesy Smithsonian Institution.

propeller. Pilcher is also credited as the first to install wheels and a spring suspension as an aid to landing and ground handling.

It should be kept in mind that Pilcher's immediate goal in powering a hang glider was to extend his flying time over that which he could obtain gliding, in order to gain more air time and perhaps experiment with a new control system to replace the weight shifting which would have been inadequate under power. His intention was to foot-launch from a hill—the engine was necessary only to sustain horizontal flight and not climb. In *The Aeronautical Annual* for 1897 Pilcher writes: "A new machine is being built which will have an oil engine to drive a screw-propeller. With this machine, without the engine, I drop 50 feet in 10 seconds—that is at the rate of 300 feet per minute. Taking my weight and the weight of the machine at 220 pounds, the work lost per minute will be about 66,000 foot-pounds per minute, or two horsepower. When I have been flown as a kite it seems that about 30 pounds pull will keep me floating at a speed of about 2,200 feet per minute, or 25 miles an hour. 30 x 2,200 = 66,000 foot-pounds = 2 horsepower, which comes to just the same thing."

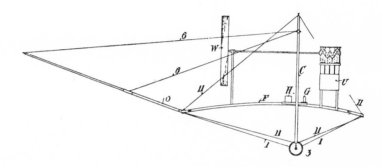

Fig. 2-11. Pilcher's drawing for a powered version of his ultralight glider, as prepared for his 1896/97 patent.

"An engine is now being made which will, I hope, exert enough power to overcome the losses arising from friction and slip, and keep the new machine floating horizontally. Of course, for the same wing surface with the extra weight of the engine, and more power than the 2 horsepower will therefore have to be used."

"Last June I happened to be in Berlin again, and Herr Lilienthal very kindly allowed me to fly off his hill with one of his double surface machines. A light steady breeze was blowing, and after practice I had no difficulty in handling his machine, but I was very much afraid that with the superposed wings high above they would prove very dangerous, especially in squally weather."

"I hope with the new machine with the engine that I shall be able to obtain results worth reporting in your next Annual, but we shall see what we shall see."

At the ASGB (Aeronautical Society of Great Britain) meeting of December 1897, referring to his Hawk, Pilcher said, "...this machine takes a pull of between 20 and 30 pounds to keep it in horizontal flight with me in it—I weigh about 140 pounds, the machine is about 50 pounds, that is 200 pounds. To keep that in horizontal flight with 20 pounds pull means a pull on only about one-tenth the weight of the machine." He adds later in the speech, "Now that I have learned to

Fig. 2-12. An artist's conception of Pilcher's 1899 foot-launched ultralight triplane. Courtesy Philip Jarrett, R.AeS.

handle one of these things more or less, I have got an oil engine in hand of about 4 hp, which I think should be enough to keep me in horizontal flight. The pull on a line attached to the machine is between 20 and 30 pounds, the speed at which the machine floats is about 20 or 25 miles an hour. If you multiply that out you come to about 2 or 3 hp. Consequently, I have been intending simply to put a screw propeller (60 inch diameter x 48 inch pitch), driven by an oil engine, into the machine...In this machine the screw would be placed behind me, that is to say in front of the rudder, in the after part of the machine, but right above the ground so that it cannot get injured. The engine would be placed in the front, and the shaft pass over my head. I am not quite sure whether I shall put the engine in this machine (the Hawk) or in another, but not a larger machine. I cannot handle a larger machine—it gets too cumbersome. If we put a greater weight into the machine of a certain size, it only means that to float you will have to sail faster: a limit has to come in somewhere. I have tried various machines, from 150 to 300 pounds (all-up weight), but I find about 170 seems to be about as much as one can handle."

Could Pilcher's triplane have flown under power? According to Philip Jarrett, Pilcher historian, it is doubtful the aircraft could have sustained horizontal flight. Calculations suggest a cruising speed of 30 mph which would have required about 3 thrust horsepower. While Pilcher's engine produced 4 hp, it is thought his propeller was probably about 50% efficient resulting in only 2 thrust horsepower—it being a fan blade type design.

At any rate, the triplane would have most likely been a better glider than the Hawk, and it serves as a sort of "missing link" between a hang glider and a proper ultralight airplane. Pilcher illustrated this in a speech before the Military Society of Ireland in January 1897, when he said: "The object of experimenting with soaring machines is to enable one to have practice in starting and alighting and

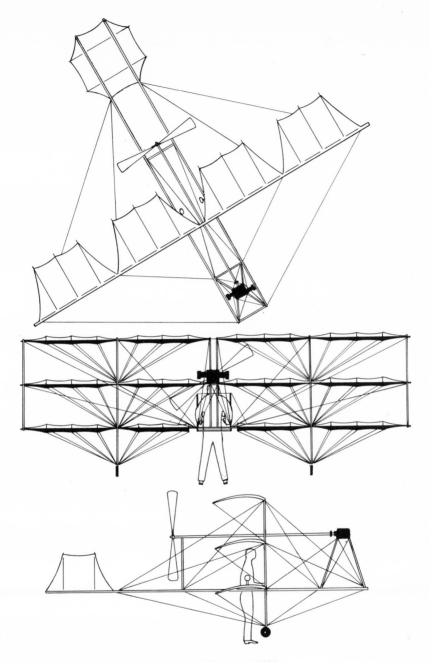

Fig. 2-13. Three-view drawing of Pilcher's Ultralight Triplane of 1899.

controlling a machine in the air. They cannot possibly float horizontally in the air for any length of time, but to keep going must necessarily lose in elevation. They are excellent schooling machines, and that is all they are meant to be, until power, in the shape of an engine working a screw propeller, or an engine working wings to drive the machine forward, is added. Then, a person who is used to sailing down a hill with a simple soaring machine will be able to fly with comparative safety. One can best compare them to bicycles having no cranks, but on which one could learn to balance by coming down an incline." Pilcher confirmed this line of thinking at the December 1897 ASGB meeting by saying "...I hope in time what are now soaring machines will develop into bona fide flying machines."

The triplane was certainly Pilcher's greatest achievement—its powered form displaying a marked similarity to the modern ultralight. We cannot help but wonder what developments would have occurred had Pilcher lived to fly his triplane.

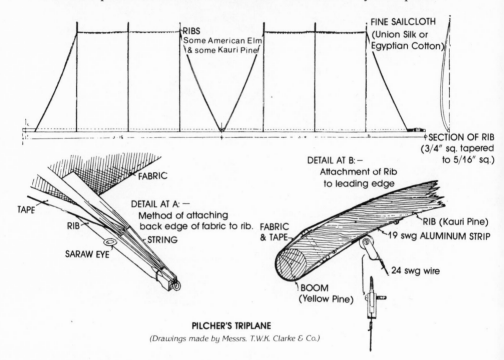

PILCHER'S TRIPLANE
(Drawings made by Messrs. T.W.K. Clarke & Co.)

Fig. 2-14. The Clarke drawing of constructional details for Pilcher's triplane.

Augustus Herring

Almost forgotten by aviation historians, Augustus M. Herring played a key role in the beginnings of the airplane and was probably the first man in history to fly a powered ultralight! He worked with Octave Chanute and Prof. Langley, made more than 1200 glides, and was considered the best hang glider pilot of his day, after Lilienthal. He invented a pitch stabilization device (elastically mounted tail) and is credited with inventing the parallel bar/armpit pilot suspension system! (Lilienthal had relied on a very uncomfortable "forearm-resting-on-airframe" method.)

An article in *Harper's Weekly,* October 24, 1908 gives us some insight of Herring's aeronautical beginnings. "From earliest boyhood, Herring was obsessed with the idea that man ought to fly." When his father asked him about a career, according to a lifelong friend, Gus replied, "I'd like to go to Stevens Institute and study engineering." When his father asked "Why?" he said. "Because I'm going to build a flying machine. You can't do that by rule of thumb. You must have exact scientific knowledge and train to conquer the air." That was in 1884, or twelve years before the Wright Brothers became interested in flying!

Hoping to graduate in 1888, the university unfortunately refused his thesis,

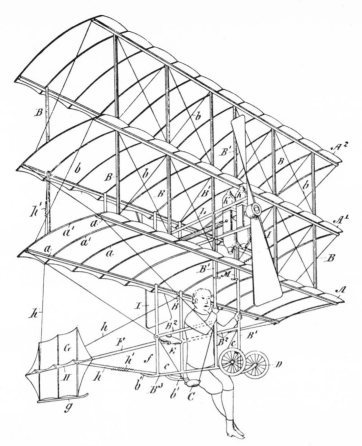

Fig. 2-15. Chanute and Herring's powered ultralight triplane design, from Moy's patent of 1897.

"The Flying Machine as a Mechanical Engineering Problem." He then agreed to another entitled "Marine Engines" which was accepted, but did not hand it in, so Herring was denied his degree. While at Stevens, he built flying models and one full-sized glider. The glider however would not carry his 150 pounds, and was wrecked.

Upon leaving Stevens, Herring continued experimenting with both rubber and steam powered models. He met with some real successes and developed a sound understanding of basic stability and power requirements.

In 1894, he built three or four modified, lighter weight versions of Lilienthal gliders employing a triangular "A-frame," typical of modern hang gliders. One even incorporated "spoilers" of some sort on the leading edges. However, they were located too close to the center section to be efficient. During this same year, Herring was put in touch with Octave Chanute who employed him to make engineering drawings and models from sketches.

Herring then wrote an article for *The American Engineer and Railroad Journal* entitled "Soaring Experiments" which was published in January 1895. This brought Herring to the attention of Dr.Langley of the Smithsonian Institution, who invited him to Washington, where he was placed in charge of Langley's experiments.

Interestingly, it was during this year at the Smithsonian that Herring convinced

Langley to give up on the flat plate wing as inferior, and return to the curved airfoil type wing. Langley's No. 5 flyer (a model) was so modified and then flew successfully several months later under Manly's (an assistant) direction.

After Herring left Langley, probably because they didn't get along too well, he joined Chanute in Chicago. Chanute and Herring experimented with model gliders for a few months, but soon decided they were of no further usefulness, so turned to full-size gliders.

The summer of 1896 saw Herring and Chanute test Herring's third modified Lilienthal-type glider, and several Chanute multi-wing designs. Chanute had Herring

Fig. 2-16. Front view of Herrings 1898 powered ultralight resting on its wheels with Herring suspended by his armpits. Courtesy Gene Husting Aeronautical Collection.

do the flight testing since he was in his 60's, while Herring was in his late 20's.

One of Chanute's gliders, the "Katydid" had up to six pairs of wings, some removable, but its performance was not too good. In the meantime, Herring built a jointly designed triplane, but the lower wing was removed because it kept catching on the sand. This modification lead to the success of the glider, which is now called the "Chanute glider" but also called the "Herring glider" by Chanute and then the "Chanute-Herring glider." This biplane, which included an elastic mounted tail (gust attenuator) is the one which inspired the Wright Brothers, according to Dr. A.F. Zahm.

In September of 1896, Herring left Chanute, but worked for him off and on during the next six or seven years. In fact, he actually rebuilt the "Katydid" and flew it at the Wright Brothers camp at Kitty Hawk in 1902. Its performance however, was far surpassed by the Wright's glider with its aerodynamic controls.

Herring had previously teamed-up with a Matthias C. Arnot a Yale-educated engineer and banker, who funded an improved version of the 1896 biplane, which

Fig. 2-17. Herring and his foot-launched ultralight, after what may have been the first flight of a powered, heavier-than-air aircraft. Courtesy Gene Husting Aeronautical Collection.

the two men tested in front of Chanute at the dunes. Aided by Arnot, Herring then built a heavier version of the "Chanute-Herring" biplane hang glider. It had a wingspan of 18 feet and a chord of 4½ feet. A horizontally opposed, two cylinder, 12 pound compressed air motor was mounted even with and just ahead of the lower wing. A shaft drove two 5 foot diameter propellers mounted in tandem—one ahead of the wings and the other behind the wings. The compressed air tank located below the wings ahead of the pilot, held 884 cubic inches and was generally filled to 600 psi. The four center section wing struts had angled in extensions below the lower wing which supported the parallel bars from which Herring hung. The tail consisted of the usual horizontal and vertical stabilizer.

On October 11, 1898, Herring made his first powered around skimming flight on the beach at St. Joseph, Michigan. He flew against a head wind of from 20 to 25 mph while travelling some 50 feet over the ground, or about 267 feet through the air. The flight was witnessed by William Engberg, the owner of the machine shop where Herring built mechanical parts for his flying machines.

No doubt ecstatic, Herring immediately contacted Octave Chanute to witness another flight on October 16. Zahm who arrived earlier was convinced the machine was capable of flight, while Chanute was skeptical. Unfortunately, Herring could not get his gas engined air compressor to run, making it impossible to fly that day. The following day saw the aircraft damaged and Chanute left believing Herring to be a fraud.

Undaunted, Herring planned another attempt for October 22, and called together news reporters, Arnot and the machine shop owner. The morning air was cool with a stiff breeze, of about 26 mph blowing off the lake. Herring and company went to an old pavilion on the beach, while some young boys watched from behind the bushes. A beachside hot dog stand was opened.

Herring removed the fuselage and wing assemblies from the pavilion and assembled them on the beach. He started the air compressor's gasoline engine, attached the hose to the aircraft's tank, filling it with compressed air. Detaching the hose, he crawled under the biplane and lifted it off the sand. He positioned himself for the takeoff run and opened the air valve. The motor buzzed to life, turning the propellers faster and faster. Herring leaned forward into the breeze and was airborne in a couple of quick steps, the flight lasted from 8 to 10 seconds and covered about 75 feet over the sand, at a height of a foot or two or 350 feet through the air. If the compressed air tank had been larger, who knows how far he might have flown!

Satisfied he had proven the feasibility of powered flight, Herring immediately began work on a light weight steam engine. He also rented an old iron works and began working on a larger machine, with which he hoped to make flights of longer duration. After two years and $25,000 were spent on the project, a fire completely destroyed everything in 1899.

Then in May 1900, Chanute responded to a letter from Wilbur Wright, asking for his ideas on the construction of a flying machine, the materials to use, the best place to experiment, etc. He said it was his desire to construct a flying machine and had some ideas of his own, particularly regarding control. Chanute then sent him all the information he had, which was the beginning of a long and continued correspondence.

Fig. 2-18, Herring's compressed air motor as used on his biplane. "The Aeronautical Annual," 1897.

Herring later went on to arrange for the financing and organized the first company in the U.S. to manufacture airplanes, the Herring-Curtiss company.

It should also be mentioned that Chanute and Herring made a patent application in 1896 for a motorized triplane hang glider. It was granted in England and France, but not the U.S. The patent examiner, a Mr. W.W. Townsend, stated in a letter dated January 4, 1898, that "the entire invention rests on a theory that has never been proven." Ironically, the Director of Patents in 1910 said that there was never any valid reason Herring's patent could not have been granted as late as 1907, after the Wright's accomplishments had been accepted, but 1910 was too late!

Fig. 2-19. Herring's two-cylinder gasoline engine was unfortunately destroyed in a workshop fire.

The Wright Brothers

As is well known, the Wright Brothers are credited with inventing the airplane. And well they should be, for it was they, and they alone, who literally "put-it-all-together." Their "Kitty Hawk Flyer" embodied all the essentials needed to make it a success. While experimenters previously discussed relied on weight shift for control, it was the Wrights who developed the true three-axis aerodynamic control system—the heart of their patent and all successful flying machines. Not until after they had mastered the control of their ultralight gliders, (the biggest ever flown) did they even consider power. When they finally did apply power they felt quite confident of their eventual success. While it is true that all the Wright aircraft from their "Flyer" on, except for a 1911 glider, were not ultralight, their invention is basic to all aircraft flying today.

The Wrights' own account of that glorious day in 1903 is worth reading.

"On the morning of December 17th, between the hours of 10:30 o'clock and noon, four flights were made, two by Mr. Orville Wright and two by Mr. Wilbur Wright. The starts were all made from a point on the level and about 200 feet west of our camp which is located a quarter of a mile south of the Kill Devil Sand Hill, in Dare County, North Carolina.

The wind at the time of the flights had a velocity of twenty-seven miles an hour at ten o'clock, and twenty-four miles an hour at noon, as recorded by the anemometer at the Kitty Hawk weather bureau station. This anemometer is thirty feet from the ground. Our own measurements, made with a hand anemometer at a height of four feet from the ground, showed a velocity of about twenty-two miles when the first flight was made, and twenty and a half miles at the time of the last one. The flights were directly against the wind.

Each time the machine started from the level ground by its own power alone, with no assistance from gravity or an other sources whatever. After a run of about forty feet along a monorail track, which held the machine eight inches from the

Fig. 2-20. Wilbur Wright in the brothers' 1902 ultralight glider in which they perfected the three-axis aerodynamic control system — the heart of their "flying machine" patent.

ground, it rose from the track and under the direction of the operator, climbed upward on an inclined course till a height of eight or ten feet from the ground was reached, after which the course was kept as near horizontal as the wind gusts and the limited skill of the operator would permit.

Into the teeth of a December gale the "Flyer" made its way forward with a speed of ten miles an hour over the ground, and thirty to thirty-five miles an hour through the air. It had previsouly been decided that, for reasons of personal safety, these first trials would be made as close to the ground as possible. The height chosen was scarcely sufficient for maneuvering in so gusty a wind and with no previous acquaintance with the conduct of the machine and its controlling mechanisms. Consequently the first flight was short.

The succeeding flights rapidly increased in length and at the fourth trial a flight of fifty-nine seconds was made, in which time the machine flew a little more than a half mile through the air, and a distance of 852 feet over the ground. The landing was due to a slight error of judgment on the part of the operator. After passing over a little hummock of sand, in attempting to bring the machine down to the desired height, the operator turned the rudder [elevator] too far, and the machine turned downward more quickly than had been expected. The reverse movement of the rudder was a fraction of a second too late to prevent the machine from touching the ground and thus ending the flight. The whole occurrence occupied little, if any more, than one second of time.

Only those who are acquainted with practical aeronautics can appreciate the difficulties of attempting the first trials of a flying machine in a twenty-five-mile

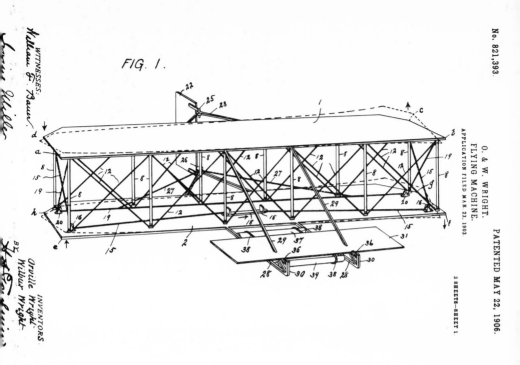

No. 821,393.

O. & W. WRIGHT.
FLYING MACHINE.
APPLICATION FILED MAR. 23, 1903.

PATENTED MAY 22, 1906.

3 SHEETS—SHEET 1.

FIG. 1.

WITNESSES:
William F. Baum.

INVENTORS
Orville Wright
Wilbur Wright
BY

Fig. 2-21. Patent drawing for the Wright Brothers flying machine, featuring their three-axis control system.

Fig. 2-22. The moment of triumph. Orville Wright lifts off the world's first manned, powered and controlled flight of a heavier-than-air aircraft as Wilbur looks on with intensity. "Flyer" was powered by homemade 12 hp, four cylinder, four cycle engine turning two pusher propellers via chain drive reduction. Courtesy Smithsonian Institution.

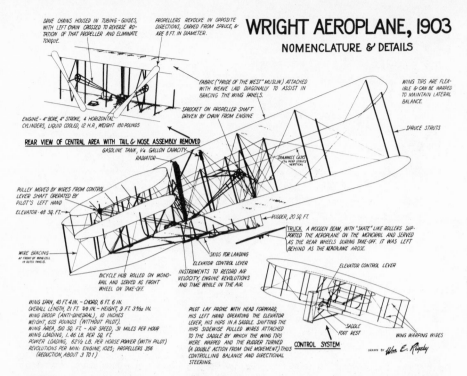

WRIGHT AEROPLANE, 1903
NOMENCLATURE & DETAILS

DRIVE CHAINS HOUSED IN TUBING - GUIDES, WITH LEFT CHAIN CROSSED TO REVERSE ROTATION OF THAT PROPELLER AND ELIMINATE TORQUE.

PROPELLERS REVOLVE IN OPPOSITE DIRECTIONS, CARVED FROM SPRUCE, & ARE 8 FT. IN DIAMETER.

FABRIC ("PRIDE OF THE WEST" MUSLIN) ATTACHED WITH WEAVE LAID DIAGONALLY TO ASSIST IN BRACING THE WING PANELS.

WING TIPS ARE FLEXIBLE & CAN BE WARPED TO MAINTAIN LATERAL BALANCE.

SPROCKET ON PROPELLER SHAFT DRIVEN BY CHAIN FROM ENGINE

ENGINE - 4" BORE, 4" STROKE, 4 HORIZONTAL CYLINDERS, LIQUID COOLED, 12 H.P., WEIGHT 180 POUNDS

SPRUCE STRUTS

REAR VIEW OF CENTRAL AREA WITH TAIL & NOSE ASSEMBLY REMOVED

GASOLINE TANK, 1/4 GALLON CAPACITY.
RADIATOR

TRAVERSE GUYS (TO KEEP STRUTS VERTICAL)

PULLEY MOVED BY WIRES FROM CONTROL LEVER SHAFT OPERATED BY PILOT'S LEFT HAND
ELEVATOR - 48 SQ. FT.

RUDDER, 20 SQ. FT.

TRUCK. A WOODEN BEAM, WITH "SKATE" LIKE ROLLERS SUPPORTED THE AEROPLANE ON THE MONORAIL AND SERVED AS THE REAR WHEELS DURING TAKE-OFF. IT WAS LEFT BEHIND AS THE AEROPLANE AROSE.

WIRE BRACING AT FRONT OF WING CELL IN OUTER PANELS.

SKIDS FOR LANDING

ELEVATOR CONTROL LEVER

BICYCLE HUB ROLLED ON MONORAIL AND SERVED AS FRONT WHEEL ON TAKE-OFF.

INSTRUMENTS TO RECORD AIR VELOCITY, ENGINE REVOLUTIONS AND TIME WHILE IN THE AIR.

ELEVATOR CONTROL LEVER

WING SPAN, 40 FT. 4 IN. - CHORD, 6 FT. 6 IN.
OVERALL LENGTH, 21 FT. 3/8 IN. - HEIGHT, 9 FT. 3 5/32 IN.
WING DROOP (ANTI-DIHEDRAL), 10 INCHES
WEIGHT, 605 POUNDS (WITHOUT PILOT).
WING AREA, 510 SQ. FT. - AIR SPEED, 31 MILES PER HOUR
WING LOADING, 1.46 LB. PER SQ. FT.
POWER LOADING, 62 1/2 LB. PER HORSE POWER (WITH PILOT)
REVOLUTIONS PER MIN: ENGINE, 1025; PROPELLERS 356
(REDUCTION, ABOUT 3 TO 1)

PILOT LAY PRONE WITH HEAD FORWARD, HIS LEFT HAND OPERATING THE ELEVATOR LEVER, HIS HIPS IN A SADDLE. SHIFTING THE HIPS SIDEWISE PULLED WIRES ATTACHED TO THE SADDLE BY WHICH THE WING TIPS WERE WARPED AND THE RUDDER TURNED (A DOUBLE ACTION FROM ONE MOVEMENT) THUS CONTROLLING BALANCE AND DIRECTIONAL STEERING.

SADDLE
FOOT REST
WING WARPING WIRES

CONTROL SYSTEM

DRAWN BY Wm. E. Rigsby

Fig. 2-23. Details and nomenclature of the Wright Brothers Kitty Hawk Flyer. Courtesy Smithsonian Institution.

gale. As winter was already well set in, we should have postponed our trials to a more favorable season, but for the fact that we were determined, before returning home, to know whether the machine possessed sufficient power to fly, sufficient

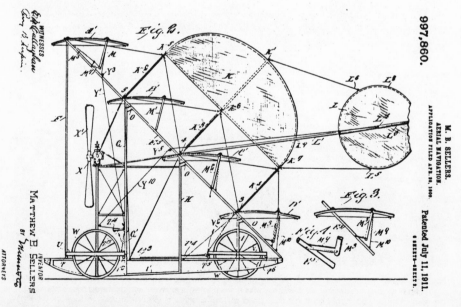

Fig. 2-24. Patent drawing for Mathew Sellers quadruplane.

strength to withstand the shock of landings, and sufficient capacity of control to make flight safe in boisterous winds, as well as in calm air. When these points had been definitely established we at once packed our goods and returned home, knowing that the age of the flying machine had come at last."

Matthew Sellers

Very little has ever been published about this unusual ultralight built and flown by Sellers in Kentucky during 1908. His patent drawing is shown for reference, as well as a photograph.

Fig. 2-25. Mathew Sellers 1908 quadruplane was the first ultralight to fly in the United States. Courtesy Smithsonian Institution.

A. V. Roe

"When Roe began trial taxiing runs with the Antoinette engine, he found that the extra power of the engine was too much for the propeller.

One morning as he travelled faster than he had ever done down the track, the engine suddenly started to race, and the biplane stopped. He switched off the motor and hurried round to the back of the machine. The propeller blades were missing. He bent to examine the boss, and ducked quickly. For a moment he had the ludicrous notion that someone had thrown something at him. He turned angrily towards the hedge, but the track was deserted. Then, a few feet away, he saw the blade of the propeller, which had spun into the air and circled back like a boomerang.

The trouble with the propeller recurred. As the engine neared its maximum power, the force of the increasing speed of the revolutions regularly spun the propeller off the boss.

Roe hammered in more and more plugs, but it was some days before he was satisfied that the trouble was solved. After one or two trial runs he resumed the taxiing tests, gradually increasing speed until the front wheels actually lifted off the ground. The propeller held firm.

That night the weather was fine, and to save the trouble of putting the machine back into the shed, he left it outside, secured to trestles.

Next morning, June 8th, 1908, he was up as usual at daybreak.

With his customary precision and thoroughness he checked over the machine, the struts and bracings, the bolts and couplings, spars and fabrics. He started the engine. A staccato clacking broke the quiet of the early morning: a thin piping clatter compared with the noise of modern aero engines.

He climbed into his seat, an open perch of two crossbars and a back rest. Knees up, he placed his feet on the steering rod which was wired to the front wheel axle. Pressing forward alternatively with his right and left foot, he checked that the wheels changed direction in response to the movements.

He tested the operation of the flying control, tilting and twisting the elevator. Satisfied, he opened the throttle slowly. Quivering and shaking, the Roe I biplane ran towards a horizon bright with the gold of the sunrise.

Although the fact that the front wheels had lifted on previous occasions was evidence that he must be on the verge of achieving flight, Roe had no conscious thought that this day, this time, he was going to fly. In any case it is doubtful

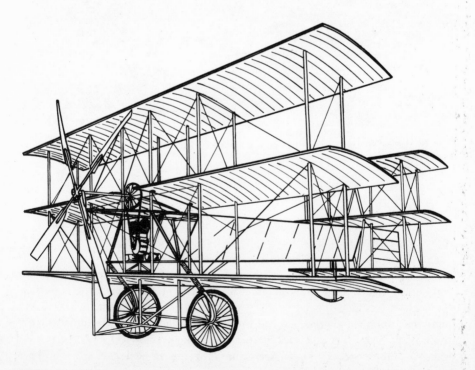

Fig. 2-26. A. V. Roe's "Bullseye" ultralight triplane of 1909 was first successful airplane flown in England. Had 9 hp engine and reduction drive propeller.

whether he would have bothered to arrange for observers to be present to record his flight officially.

The prospect of making his first flight, once a dream complete in itself that had occupied all his thoughts and sacrifice for five years, had acquired a new perspective. For months, he had been so sure of his ability to fly that he had ceased to think of flight in terms of leaving the ground. He had gone to Brooklands the previous autumn not merely to rise in the air but to fly with purpose, to make a circuit of the race-track and win the reward of much needed prize money. The run down the track that June morning was just one more in an endless series of trials and experiments.

The track blurred between his legs, and the thrust of quickening speed tugged and pulled at the wing surfaces. He tilted the front elevator. The under surface caught the force of the airstream, braking the machine's acceleration with a jerk. Then the elevator lifted, and pulled the front wheels off the ground.

Like an animal raised unnaturally on its hind legs, the machine raced forward. Holding the flying control right back in the climbing position, and the engine at full power, Roe watched the ground racing beneath him.

It was hard to tell the exact instant when the back wheels left the ground; and it took moments of incredulous surprise before he fully realized the fact that the aeroplane was unmistakably free of the earth. Then he noticed the change in the note of the engine, the drop in vibration, the feel of the air buffeting beneath him as though he were floating on the crests of billowing waves.

He was flying. Nothing else mattered. All the hardships and struggles found their full reward in that moment of elation and contentment. Everything had fallen into place. Life for him had found its meaning. In breaking free from the earth, he had broken free also of all the bonds of frustration and disappointment that had so long held him back. Now his path was ahead. He was going forward." (From A.V. Roe by Edward Lanchberry, London: Bodley Head, 1956)

The Roe I biplane was little more than an ultralight, weighing in at 600 pounds gross. It was variously powered by first a 9 hp, then a 24 hp engine, and is considered the first English aircraft to fly. Mr. Roe's second airplane, The Roe II triplane, was truly an ultralight. It too, was variously powered by engines ranging from a 6 hp JAP to a 24 hp Antoinette. It had a wingspan of 20 ft., wing area of 320 sq. ft. and empty and loaded weights of 200 pounds.

Santos-Dumont

Santos-Dumont probably deserves more credit than anyone else of his time for getting ultralight aviation started. After spending several years building and flying dirigibles, this little Brazilian living in Paris turned his thoughts towards ultralights. In 1906, he became the first man in Europe to fly. Three years later, he came out with his diminutive "Demoiselle." It cruised at 56 mph, and could lift its 260 pounds plus pilot off the ground in only about 200 feet.

True to form and unlike his contemporaries, Santos released his drawings to the general public. In fact, *Popular Mechanics* published a complete set of working drawings in their June and July, 1910 issues. The magazine made the following statement:

"From time to time vague descriptions of the manner of constructing aeroplanes

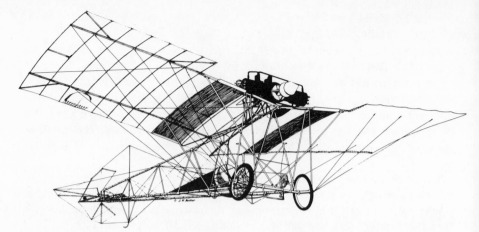

Fig. 2-27. Santos-Dumont's 1909 Demoiselle was first popular ultralight. Copyright J. W. Batter, "WWI Aero" magazine.

have been given to the public. All over the United States there are thousands of persons who are intensely interested in the subject of aerial flight, but until now nothing of a tangible nature has been presented on which work could be started with a reasonable prospect of success. It is a great satisfaction therefore, to be able to present the working drawings of the wonderful monoplane invented by M. Santos-Dumont. However, it would be useless for anyone not possessed of some mechanical skill, and plenty of common sense, to attempt to construct a copy of the famous flyer, even with such detailed drawings and instructions."

Excerpts from the *Popular Mechanics* feature follow.

"Following the announcement, made some months ago by Alberto Santos-Dumont that he intended to give the plans of his latest aeroplane, the Demoiselle, to the world in the interest of aeronautics, great interest has been centered in the wonderful monoplane. It is the lightest and smallest of all heavier-than-air machines, yet is thoroughly practical.

"It would be well, of course, for the prospective aviator to make himself acquainted with the subject of the atmosphere as it applies to aeronautics, to have a good knowledge of gasoline motors, and to study the properties and qualities of the different materials which enter into construction of the monoplane.

"The greatest items of expense will be the motor and the propeller. Santos-Dumont used a Darracq motor of 30 hp. There are American motors which will do just as well, probably. We advise that the propeller be purchased.

"A good place to start would be the vertical rudder, plate iii. the thickness of the bamboo there given is the maximum. The heavier and stronger portions are used for the centers where the strain is heaviest. Drawing C on this plate shows the manner in which the cloth is attached to the framework by No. 21 piano wire, as it should be done throughout.

"After having sewn the piano wire into the outer edge of the cloth, the wire should be stretched to get it to the extremity, and then dropped into a slot made for it to rest in on the outer end of the bamboo. Thus the pieces of cloth are well stretched, and are held firmly in place, adding to the strength of the machine. This applies to the wings also, where every added bit of strength and firmness adds to the successful completion.

Fig. 2-28. The Demoiselle featured a universal jointed all-moving tail and wing warping. Twin-cylinder opposed Duthell-Chalmers engine produced 20 hp directly to prop. Courtesy Smithsonian Institution.

"Slots are made at the ends of the bamboos for the wires to slip into. It is a good idea to put a cork into the hollow end and cut the slots in both at the same time. Brass wire, gauge No. 25, should be wound around the rod just below the end of the slot to prevent its splitting. In later models, Santos-Dumont used metal caps over the ends of the bamboo rods.

"The cloth used by Santos-Dumont was a very finely woven silk. It has the greatest objection of expense, however, and it would probably be as well to use percale or muslin of the best grade.

"Plate IV shows the details of the horizontal rudder which governs the altitude of the machine 'Gouvernail de Profondeur' is the French term for it. It should be constructed in the same manner as the vertical rudder. The method of attaching the rudders to the frame is shown on Plate IV. This is practically a universal joint, allowing the steering device to be turned in any direction by the controlling wires shown on Plate I. These wires should be very carefully selected and tested, for a great deal depends upon their strength. It would be very imprudent to use ordinary piano wire. The U-joint should be made of the best steel tubing procurable; good bicycle tubing is excellent.

"Having finished the steering arrangement, it would be wise to take up construction of the wings next. These are made entirely of bamboo rods with bamboo or ash spars as shown in Plate V. However, Clement Bayard, at whose factory in France these monoplanes are being manufactured, makes the spars of poplar or ash. Aluminum tubes also have been used. It would be advisable, however, to stick to the bamboo rods which served Santos-Dumont so well.

"In order to secure the ribbing curves as shown at the top of Plate V, it would be sufficient to bend the rods over a form by force. They may also be bent by means of a string tied to the ends, drawing them together, and then plunging them into boiling water for about 15 minutes. They will retain their shape if given time to dry before the strings are removed. If the builder desires to use wood, he may proceed in like manner. The curve is almost the true arc of a circle. The whole plane structure is kept rigid by guide wires running to the frame as shown in Plate I.

"The wings completed, it would be well next to undertake construction of the frame. The wheels are easily made, for, save that they have a longer hub, they are very similar in construction to the ordinary bicycle wheel.

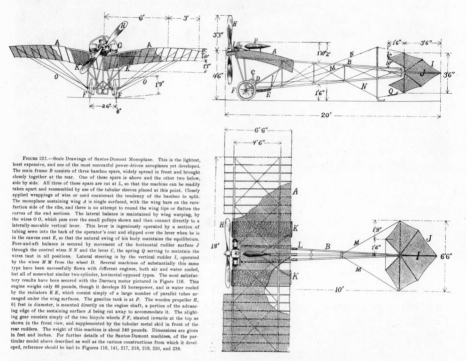

FIGURE 221.—Scale Drawings of Santos-Dumont Monoplane. This is the lightest, least expensive, and one of the most successful power-driven aeroplanes yet developed. The main frame B consists of three bamboo spars, widely spread in front and brought closely together at the rear. One of these spars is above and the other two below, side by side. All three of these spars are cut at L, so that the machine can be readily taken apart and reassembled by use of the tubular sleeves placed at this point. Closely applied wrappings of wire or cord counteract the tendency of the bamboo to split. The monoplane sustaining wing A is single surfaced, with the wing bars on the rarefaction side of the ribs, and there is no attempt to round the wing tips or flatten the curves of the end sections. The lateral balance is maintained by wing warping, by the wires O O, which pass over the small pulleys shown and then connect directly to a laterally-movable vertical lever. This lever is ingeniously operated by a section of tubing sewn into the back of the operator's coat and slipped over the lever when he is in the canvas seat E, so that the natural swing of his body maintains the equilibrium. Fore-and-aft balance is secured by movement of the horizontal rudder surface J through the control wires N N and the lever C, the spring Q serving to maintain the wires taut in all positions. Lateral steering is by the vertical rudder I, operated by the wires M M from the wheel D. Several machines of substantially this same type have been successfully flown with different engines, both air and water cooled, but all of somewhat similar two-cylinder, horizontal-opposed types. The most satisfactory results have been secured with the Darracq motor pictured in Figure 116. This engine weighs only 66 pounds, though it develops 35 horsepower, and is water cooled by the radiators K K, which consist simply of a large number of parallel tubes arranged under the wing surfaces. The gasoline tank is at P. The wooden propeller H, 6½ feet in diameter, is mounted directly on the engine shaft, a portion of the advancing edge of the sustaining surface A being cut away to accommodate it. The alighting gear consists simply of the two bicycle wheels F F, slanted inwards at the top as shown in the front view, and supplemented by the tubular metal skid in front of the rear rudders. The weight of this machine is about 240 pounds. Dimensions are given in feet and inches. For further details of the Santos-Dumont machines, of the particular model above described as well as the various constructions from which it developed, reference should be had to Figures 116, 141, 217, 218, 219, 220, and 238.

Fig. 2-29. Three-view drawing of the Demoiselle. From "Vehicles of the Air", Loughhead, 1911.

"It would be well to use strong spokes, for at times, when the machine strikes the ground suddenly, great stress is put upon them. Santos-Dumont settled on a wheel hub length of six inches. These hubs are simply slipped on over the axle tubes and fastened with a cotter pin. It is not necessary to provide any special bearings for the wheels, as it is intended they should work with a slight friction. The wheels are inclined toward one another at the top, to prevent their being broken when subjected to a light jar. Details of construction of the joints, where the landing gear tubing is attached to the bamboo frame, are shown in Detail of Assembly A on Plate VII. It would be imprudent and dangerous to make a hole in any of the three main bamboo rods which constitute the frame of the machine, for this would detract from their strength.

"The machine thus far completed, we may proceed to attach the piano wire stretchers, and then the wires controlling the horizontal and vertical rudders and governing the warping of the planes. The rudder controls may be installed in accordance with the builder's ideas, and the motor controls will vary, of course, with the type of motor used.

"In Santos-Dumont's Demoiselle, the wire regulating the horizontal rudder is attached to a lever within easy reach of the pilot's right hand. The vertical rudder is controlled by a wheel at the pilot's left hand.

"The lever which controls the warping of the planes is placed behind the pilot's seat. Santos-Dumont operated this by bending his body to the right or left, the lever fitting into a tube fastened to his coat in the rear. A side movement pulls the rear end of the wing opposite to the side to which the pilot leans. The balancing of the whole apparatus is, therefore, in a manner, automatic. The pilot has but to bend over to one side in order to balance the machine.

"Springs are introduced on the wires which control the rudders of some of the machines, so as to bring the rudder back to its normal position without effort on

Fig. 2-30. Santos Dumont takes to the air in the spring of 1909 at St. Cyr, France. Courtesy Smithsonian Institution.

the part of the operator. The seat is a piece of canvas or leather stretched across the two lower bamboo rods just behind the wheels.

"Santos-Dumont had his motor control so arranged that he could regulate the supply of gasoline by his foot. The spark switch may be placed on the steering lever, or may be arranged differently with other motors. It is of prime importance that the motor should be perfectly balanced, direct-connected to the axle holding the propeller. The gasoline reservoir is located behind the pilot's seat, the fuel being forced up into a smaller one just above the motor.

"In his remarkable flight from St. Cyr to Buc, the inventor of the monoplane used a two-cylinder Darracq of 30 hp which gave the propeller 1000 rpm. It weighed just over 99 pounds. The entire machine weighed 260 pounds without the pilot. . ."

Working Drawings of the "Demoiselle"

SANTOS-DUMONT'S
Remarkable Aeroplane

Price $2.00 Postpaid

The Smallest Flyer Ever Built

One of the Most Successful

Complete plans for the construction of the wonderful monoplane offered to the public for the first time.

The machine is unencumbered by patent rights, the famous aviator preferring to place his invention at the disposal of the world in the interest of the art to which he has devoted his life. These plans are published in two parts, in the June and July numbers of Popular Mechanics Magazine, but the restrictions of space make them much smaller. They were secured by representatives of Popular Mechanics from Santos-Dumont, and are the result of consultations with his engineers and observations made at his workshops.

The set comprises seven large blue prints, showing every detail of construction, accompanied by a description of how to build.

POPULAR MECHANICS COMPANY
225 Washington Street, CHICAGO, ILLINOIS

Fig. 2-31. A 1910 advertisement for the Demoiselle as published in "Popular Mechanics" magazine.

HUNTINGTON TYPE H-12 MOTORCYCLE ENGINE MONOPLANE

SPECIFICATIONS

General Dimensions

Wing span.....................20 ft.
Length over all.............14 ft. 6 in.
Height over all ....54 in.
Wing chord ....54 in.
Wing section..................U.S.A. 4
Angle of incidence .... 4°
Dihedral........................ 1°

Areas

Wing area (including ailerons).80 sq. ft.
Ailerons ....11 sq. ft.
Stabilizer ....5.6 sq. ft.
Elevators....................6 sq. ft.
Rudder......................4 sq. ft.

Power Plant

2 Cyl. air cooled V type engine 12-15 h.p.
Weight w. magneto & carbureter 85 lbs.

Weights

Machine empty ....220 lbs.
Fuel and oil .... 30 lbs.
Pilot ....150 lbs.
Useful load ....180 lbs.
Total weight...................400 lbs.
Percent of useful load 45%
Wing loadings ....5 lbs per sq. in.
Power loading...........30 lbs. per h.p.

Performance (Computed 12 h.p.)

High speed near sea level .....60 m.p.h.
Cruising speed ....52 m.p.h.
Landing speed ....32 m.p.h.
Range at cruising speed–5 hrs...250 mls.
Initial climb............240 ft. per min.
Ceiling ....7,500 ft.
Factor of safety................... 8

The monoplane type was chosen not only because of its unequaled efficiency but also because of its greater safety, reliability and lower cost, due to the fact that fewer parts are required in its construction. For these reasons we are confident that we are offering the safest, simplest and most efficient airplane that can be bought for many times our price.

The light weight of the H-12 as well as its very low resistance allow it to accelerate quickly, climb fast and get out of small fields. The low landing speed adds to the safety and increases the pleasures of cross country flying by permitting the use of almost any field, or even a country road, as an airdrome.

Good vision—an important consideration in any plane—is afforded the pilot of an H-12 thru windows cut in the sides of the fuselage, permitting him to look downward either side (he can see his wheels for landing) and by bending over slightly he can look out under the wings to either side.

Demountability is one of the many meritorious features of rigid bracing and in this instance makes it possible for one person to assemble or take down the wings in five minutes, easily. The space required with the wings dismantled is only 4x14 feet, so that the housing problem holds no difficulties.

FUSELAGE: is of good streamline form, of sufficient depth to protect pilot and afford comfortable seating and control arrangements. Fuselage is rigidly braced by veneer struts, no wires being used. This feature obviates the necessity for constant truing up and does away with a large number of expensive parts such as fittings, turnbuckles, shackles, pins, etc. Aluminum cowling is provided around the engine and an aluminum fire wall reduces danger from fire to an absolute minimum.

WINGS have the U .S. A. 4 aerofoil section which gives very high lift and remarkable efficiency. They are built up according to the best practice using spruce spars and I section ribs of basswood. The wings are braced externally, to the lower fuselage longerons, by four struts which are identical and interchangeable. Wire bracing is provided in line of the structure. This system is stronger than the usual biplane bracing and requires no lining up. Wings, fuselage and control surfaces are covered with a good grade of unbleached muslin that has been found to possess ample strength and good lasting qualities and is, at the same time, quite inexpensive.

UNDERCARRIAGE is of the widely used type consisting of two vee struts of spruce, 20" wheels and tires are used, the wheels being covered to reduce their resistance. Rubber cord is used for shock absorbers and hard wire for bracing. The spacer strut is of thick aerofoil section and not only streamlines the axle but also exerts considerable lifting force.

TAIL UNIT comprises stabilizers, elevators and a balanced rudder of pleasing outline. No vertical fin is required. All surfaces are of the flat type and large enough to give positive action at very low speeds. Stabilizers are adjustable for longitudinal balance.

CONTROLS are of the conventional stick and foot bar type, the latter actuating the rubber. Stick and rock shaft are of steel tubing, the former being provided with a neat rubber grip. Aluminum pulleys and flexible cable insure smooth running. Spark and throttle control mounted on strut to left of pilot, magneto switch on dashboard.

POWER PLANT. Altho designed originally for a motorcycle engine of 12 HP the H-12 is amply strong enough to take any engine up to 30 HP and under 150 pounds, weight. The more power of course, the better the performance. Aircooled engines of the two cylinder opposed type, such as the Lawrance A-3, and of the two cylinder vee type are best, but almost any light engine may be installed with good results. Gravity feed is provided for gasoline. Capacity—gas, 4 gallons, oil, one-half gallon.

Fig. 2-32. An advertisement for the 1919 Huntington motorcycle-engined ultralight.

47

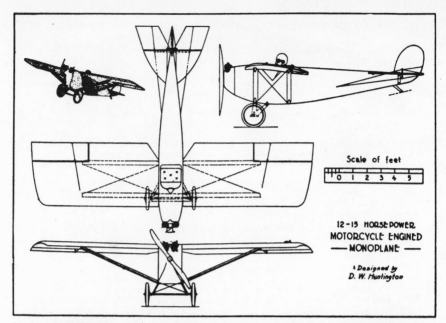

Scale of feet

12-15 HORSEPOWER
MOTORCYCLE ENGINED
— MONOPLANE —

Designed by
D. W. Huntington

BLUEPRINTS. Our complete set of prints for building the H-12 comprises four large sheets—over forty square feet of detailed drawings showing exactly how all parts are made and assembled. By making the drawings large we were able to show all assemblies quarter size and the details for the most part, full size. The very best engineering practice has been followed and it is difficult to realize how the set could be made clearer. The prices of the complete set, which also includes any special data in the form of sketches or instructions concerning powerplant installation or upon any point not thoroly understood in the plans, is $5 prepaid.

MATERIALS supplied by us are of the best quality obtainable and guaranteed. All spruce and veneer is selected stock. All bolts, nuts, tie rods and clevis pins are three and one-half per cent nickel steel, screws and nails are brass and tacks are copper. Let us quote on any materials you require.

PROPELLERS can be supplied at reasonable prices depending upon size. We shall be pleased to quote on your requirements.

BILL OF MATERIAL including woodwork roughed out, sheet steel for fittings, tanks, and all other materials used in the plane except engine and propeller—$165.
(Above price subject to two per cent cash discount only.)

KNOCK DOWN PLANE including all finished parts in the following price list, all ready to assemble quickly from our blueprints, complete except engine and propeller. Special price subject to two per cent cash discount only—$345.

PLANE built up ready to install engine and propeller, complete except those items—$765.
(Above price subject to two per cent cash discount only.)

TERMS. On all orders less than $50 cash with order. $50 or over twenty-five per cent with order, balance on delivery. All prices are f. o. b. Hempstead and include packing. Where shipping charges are sent with order any excess will be promptly refunded.

DISCOUNT. A discount of ten per cent is allowed on all orders of $20 and over. On all orders of $50 and over a further discount of two per cent will be allowed for cash in full with order.

GUARANTEE. We guarantee all materials and parts we handle to be fully adequate for the uses for which they are intended. Any parts not found as represented will be replaced free of charge or money refunded, as preferred.

YOU may use this price list when ordering and save time by merely checking the items wanted and forwarding same together with your remittance. In that case we will gladly send you another copy of the price list.

PARTS AND ACCESSORIES

FUSELAGE METAL PARTS				
164 Rudder hinge clips (2)	$ .42	356 Sta. 1 upper outer 1R-1L	1.80
299 Aluminum fire wall	3.12	357 Sta. 1 upper inner 1R-1L	.60
332 Tail Skid axle clip (2)	.54	358 Sta. 1 lower outer 1R-1L	1.80
335 Oil tank straps (2)	.30	359 Sta. 1 lower inner 1R-1L	.60
336 Gas tank straps (2)	.45	360 Sta. 2 upper outer 1R-1L	2.25
338 Gas tank straps anchors (2)	.72	361 Sta. 2 upper inner 1R-1L	.60
353 Aileron pulley fittings (2)	.45	363 Sta. 2 lower outer 1R-1L	5.70
		364 Sta. 2 lower inner 1R-1L	.60

Fig. 2-33. Continuation of the Huntington ultralight ad.

48

Huntington

Immediately following WWI, this skilled draftsman from the Curtiss Airplane Co., put the finishing touches on his ultralight—the first truly professional design in America. He sold beautifully detailed plans for $5 and even supplied kits including hard-to-find items such as fittings, wheels, aluminum, cloth, dope, glue—everything.

A portion of the H-12 brochure is reproduced above.

BUILD THIS MONOPLANE

The plane for the pleasure flyer who wants all the thrills of flying without the expense of a larger plane. Single seater with a short fuselage making handling easy. Wings braced with solid struts, no wires to loosen, give way or break. Shock absorbing spring wheels built part of the body. Whole plane low for balance. Everything simplified for ease of assembly. You can build one yourself from our working drawings and instal a motorcycle, cycle car or other motor of 12 to 20 H.P. Spread 22 feet, length 14 feet, weight 200 pounds. High safety factor of 12 to 1. Simple fittings. Speed with 15 H.P., 30-50 m.p.h. Designed by aeronautical engineers for sporting use and general flights. Be the first in your town to have one flying. Three ways to own one—Complete for $1365, knockdown without motor for $365, or plans $2, and build it yourself.

BUILD ONE YOURSELF

You who like to make things and save money as well—send $2 for a full set of working drawings showing all details of the monoplane with building instructions. With the plans comes a price list of everything needed. Many money saving ideas given in the instructions. Price of plans refunded if you buy a knockdown plane later.

BUY IT KNOCKDOWN

Supplied knockdown without motor for you to assemble for $365. Everything supplied except motor, including propeller, wheels, fittings, countershaft, woodwork cut, wire, cloth, dope, etc., and a set of plans and full instructions, ready for you to put together and set in your motor. The ideal way to own one. Orders filled in rotation. Terms, $65 cash, balance C.O.D.

BE THE FIRST IN YOUR TOWN—SEND YOUR ORDER NOW!

GEORGE D. WHITE CO.

Aeroplane Manufacturers

113 E. 49th St.   **Dept. 5**   **Los Angeles, Cal.**

Fig. 2-34. An advertisement for the 1920 White ultralight monoplane.

The White Monoplane

In the October, 1920 issue of *Everyday Engineering* this ad appeared for this diminutive ultralight.

The airplane featured an aerodynamically balanced rudder with no vertical fin. It was probably very tricky! The wheel spokes were quite unique in that they were actually springs, designed to absorb the shock of landing.

The Lympne Ultralight Competition

After the cessation of the hostilities of WWI, there was a great deal of interest in gliding. And, it wasn't before long that some enterprising individuals mounted small engines to their gliders, freeing them from a ground crew and the worries of landing off field. The idea was wildly accepted all over Europe!

Then, in 1923, several British organizations, manufacturers and a newspaper, joined together in offering prizes for the best British built and flown powered glider. The primary specifications for prospective entrants were: an engine no

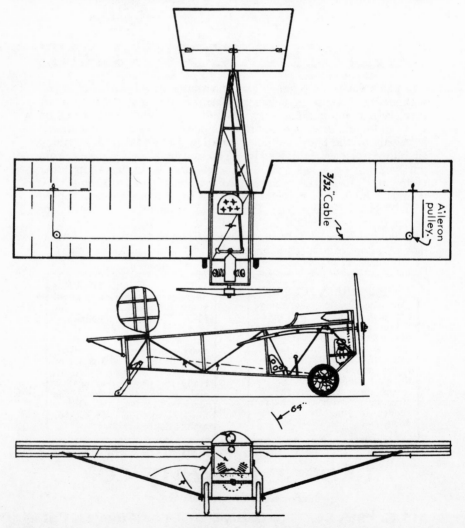

Fig. 2-35. Three-view drawing of the 1920 White monoplane. Courtesy John W. Grega.

larger than 750 cc, with the aircraft designed to be disassembled for road transport and pass through a 10 foot wide gate. No less than thirteen entrants appeared at Lympne in October 1923.

The following excerpt from NACA Technical Memorandum No. 261, May 1924, gives a good description of one of the top designs, the English Electric Wren.

The "Wren" light airplane (monoplane), entered and built by English Electric Company, two in number, competed in the mileage per gallon of gasoline contest, one tying with the A.N.E.C. making 87.5 miles, and the other finishing second with 82.5 miles. These airplanes did not take part in the competition for altitude or speed.

All parts were designed to meet the standard safety factors of the Air Ministry.

The fuselage is of the orthodox construction reinforced at points where attachment for wings, landing gear, etc., are made.

The main spars, or substantial box section, are of spruce with a special form of internal bracing which gives great torsional stiffness. The upper surface of the leading edge of the wings is covered with three-ply while the entire covering is of a special light fabric doped with Titanine glider dope and finished in aluminum.

The tailplane, elevator, fin and rudder are of substantial build, following

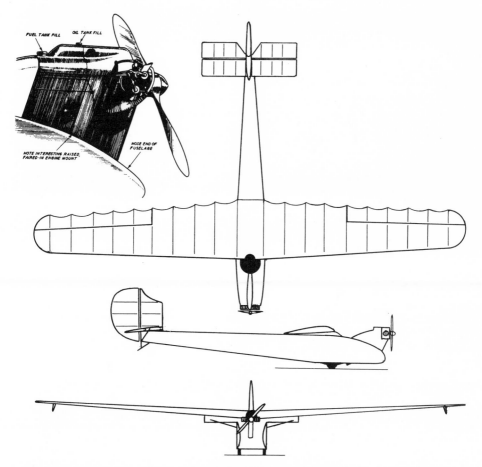

Fig. 2-36. The English Electric "Wren", a winner in the 1923 Lympne Ultralight Design Competition.

standard constructional methods. The controls, which are very efficient, also follow the approved standard practice.

The power is quite adequate for cross-country flying, except in very strong opposing winds, and is sufficient for a quick take-off from a reasonably level field. The inward position of the wheels not only reduces head resistance but enables a landing on rough or plowed fields without risk of turning over which would be almost inevitable with the usual type of landing gear.

The forward portion of the fuselage bottom is protected by a three-ply covering. This feature also serves as a braking surface and preceded by a low landing speed of 25 mph. brings the airplane to a standstill within a few yards.

The controllability is perfect even at speeds probably near 20 mph as shown in the splendid performance exhibited in the so-called "crazy flying." This airplane was not entered as a racer, the high speed being probably not over 50 mph. The engine is operated at a comparatively low speed thus insuring reliability and durability.

Mignet Flying Flea

In the summer of 1935, Mr. Henri Mignet unveiled a most curious ultralight, the infamous Pou-du-Ciel or Flying Flea. In an attempt to devise an aircraft for the man of average means and minimum flying ability, he created a sensation. The Pou-du-Ciel craze spread like wildfire beginning in France then world-wide. Mignet wrote a book, *Le Sport de l'Air* which became the bible of the sport flying

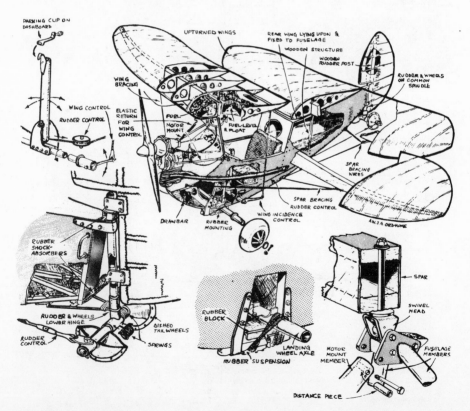

Fig. 2-37. The HM-14 "Pou-Du-Ciel" of 1935.

movement. It wasn't long before an English version was published. The British went wild too. Hundreds were being built. Mignet was in business.

Before too long however, people started getting killed. Regretable as it was, the accidents were not at first alarming. But they continued. Mignet had not thoroughly flight tested the aircraft and his trusting customers were becoming involuntary test pilots. It seems as though an uncontrollable nose down pitching moment could be established at certain angles of attack locking the little ultralight

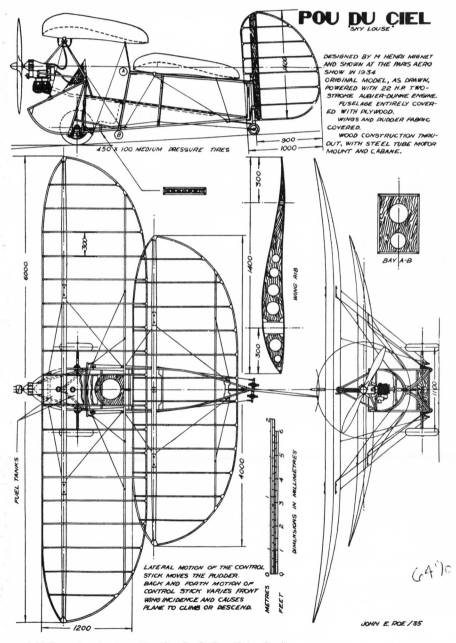

POU DU CIEL
"SKY LOUSE"

DESIGNED BY M HENRI MIGNET AND SHOWN AT THE PARIS AERO SHOW IN 1934. ORIGINAL MODEL, AS DRAWN, POWERED WITH 22 H.P. TWO-STROKE AUBIER-DUNNE ENGINE. FUSELAGE ENTIRELY COVER-ED WITH PLYWOOD. WINGS AND RUDDER FABRIC COVERED. WOOD CONSTRUCTION THRU-OUT, WITH STEEL TUBE MOTOR MOUNT AND CABANE.

450 x 100 MEDIUM PRESSURE TIRES

WING RIB

BAY A-B

FUEL TANKS

DIMENSIONS IN MILLIMETRES

METRES   FEET

LATERAL MOTION OF THE CONTROL STICK MOVES THE RUDDER. BACK AND FORTH MOTION OF CONTROL STICK VARIES FRONT WING INCIDENCE AND CAUSES PLANE TO CLIMB OR DESCEND.

JOHN E. ROE / 35

g. 2-38. Three-view drawing of the "Pou-Du-Ciel" or "Flying Flea".

into an irrecoverable dive. The Flea was banned from flying by the French Air Ministry.

Many years later the diving problem was cured and the airplane re-designed. Today, a modernized version can be built but it no longer belongs in the ultralight category, as its gross weight is now 600 pounds.

Volmer Jensen

Frustrated by a U.S. wartime ban on civil flying near the coast, the unsinkable Volmer Jensen went ahead and built a hang glider in 1941. It was patterned after the Chanute type, but only in basic configuration. Instead of relying on the archaic "body english" weight shift method of control in vogue in the late ninteenth century, Volmer went one better and put in a full three-axis, aerodynamic control system. This made the VJ-11 "solo" the first hang glider in history to be so controlled. It can still be built today from plans available from Volmer.

After the war, Volmer went back to designing powered homebuilt aircraft. He did not produce another ultralight until 1971, when he introduced the world's first fully cantilevered hang glider, the VJ-23 "Swing Wing" — a powered version of which was the first ultralight to fly the English Channel. Today he markets plans for a wheeled ultralight, the VJ-24W.

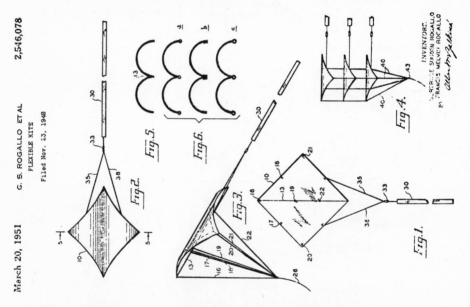

Fig. 2-39. The original Rogallo flexible wing patent — seed of the modern ultralight.

Francis M. Rogallo

Probably the single most important person in the emergence of the modern ultralight is this now retired NASA scientist. Near the end of WWII Rogallo and his wife urged NACA (predecessor of NASA) to sponsor studies that would lead to a simpler, less expensive airplane that the average worker could afford. NACA turned a deaf ear. The Rogallos decided to take it upon themselves to do the project on their own time. Their goal was to develop a rugged, inexpensive wing that could be folded when on the ground—much like those of a bat.

By 1948, they worked out something promising and filed for a U.S. patent late that year, which was finally granted in 1951. The Rogallo's patent then caught the attention of the U.S. government and they were awarded the highest bonus ever offered to individuals. The government was convinced the new kite could be used to replace the parachutes used to land spacecraft. Its main advantage over the parachute was that it could glide forward while descending. Millions were spent on research and prototype development, but the project was finally "scrubbed." Nevertheless, the concept had proven its viability and several successful man-carrying versions were flown. The modern hang glider is a direct descendent.

Ray Stits

Stits was one of sport aviation's most prolific designers from the late 40's to the mid-60's, having designed fifteen different types for home construction. Halfway through this period (1957) he got the urge to design an airplane for the "poor" pilot, planned to cost around $500.00. The result was an ultralight called the Skeeto. Needless to say, Stits was ahead of his time and his idea just didn't catch on. The following is an interesting account, in Stits's own words, of the development of the "Skeeto."

"To begin at the beginning, I would like to explain that this venture was undertaken for the purpose of developing a light, economical, home-construction kit, selling for around $500.00, which would include everything necessary to put the airplane in the air; dope, fabric, wheels, engine, prop, etc.

In turning out an aircraft kit at this price, it would be necessary to use "off the shelf industrial engines" that were already in production and being used in one form or another, and could be purchased economically and modified. Since the

Fig. 2-40. The Stits "Skeeto" ultralight of 1957 was too for ahead of its time to be accepted by the flying public.

present surplus drone engines will soon become scarce (and expensive) we decided to stay away from that type.

For ease of construction, the majority of the aircraft was wood, with chromoly tubing used at strategic locations for safety reasons. The ribs were conventional "built-up" type, ¼" cap strip, and the spars were an "I"-section using 3/16" Birch plywood, and cap strips glued at each side, tip, and bottom. The fuselage had ¾" Spruce longerons with 3/4" x 5/8" truss members and 1/8" Phillippine mahogany plywood gussets. The gussets were attached by means of a staple gun with exception of a few locations where ½" aircraft nails were used. The tail surfaces were all wood with exception of the leading edge of the rudder and elevators. ½" tubing was used for this with .035 fingers welded onto the tubing for mounting the rest of the wood members.

I find there is quite a difference in some parts of the world in what the term "Ultralight" describes. In the United States the general concensus of opinion is "any airplane" with about 30 hp or less, and with very light wing loading. While in England, France, all of Europe, Australia and New Zealand, an Ultralight is thought of as an aircraft with a gross weight of under 1200 pounds, 75 hp or less, and landing under 45 mph, which just about fits our standard light aircraft category in the U.S. For lack of better description, I'll refer to "Skeeto" as an Ultralight since it was "born" in the U.S.

After getting into the subject of powering an Ultralight, I learned why some of the early European light planes flew so well on what was supposedly low HP engines. The converted motorcycles and automobile engines used by early experimenters were rated for hp according to their bore and stroke for tax purposes, since vehicles over there were taxed according to HP, rather than weight or value, as they are over here. The ratio is roughly 3-to-1 compared to the U.S. standards for hp (550 foot pounds per minute) so the early Ultralights we read about that flew on "10 hp" actually had about 30 hp by our present standards.

In laying out the general design for the new "Skeeto," I was "aiming" for a wing loading of 3 lbs per sq. ft. at gross weight, and was planning on souping the new model, 4 hp Continental (1-cylinder, 4 cycle) to about 6 hp, and by means of a very efficient prop, hoped to get the airplane over the fence. As it turned out, the Continental engine was not in production when the aircraft was ready to go, so we substituted what was supposedly a 3½ hp, 2-cycle engine, weighing only 17 lbs. when stripped for our needs. This engine, theoretically, could be souped to about 5½ hp by winding it up, but by mounting the prop directly to the engine, we couldn't wind it above 2500 RPM.

While waiting for the Continental engine to arrive, I decided to experiment on the prop efficiency by making a V-belt reduction on the samll 2-cycle engine and reduce the prop speed about 50% (Engine installation # 2). This boosted the propulsion efficiency of the prop quite a bit and the airplane was able to taxi over the grass to almost take-off speed and would almost hold altitude when towed off with a car.

When these first test trials were made, the empty weight of the aircraft was 175 lbs, (10 lbs heavier than my estimated weight) and the wing span was 24' with a total wing area of 120 sq. ft. (At a later date I extended the wings to 30 ft.)

After further delay of the originally intended engine, I decided to try an experiment using 2 of the little 2-cycle engines V-belted to one shaft, with the prop turning about half the speed of the engines. In the meanwhile, I found that the engine I was experimenting with wasn't 3½ hp or 4 hp, but according to a graph I had received, was actually 2½ hp at 3600 rmp. By using the 2 engines V-belted to one shaft, and swinging a small handmade prop, the airplane would actually take-off and fly at about 25 mph, but in somewhat of a 3-point attitude. (Engine installation # 3).

This "compound" type engine installation didn't prove too practical because it was too heavy for the hp and the belts were slipping, so the engines were always out of synchronization, yet it met our specifications for an "off-the-shelf-engine" with a total cost of about $100.00. Deducting the hp loss from the V-belts and referring to the engine chart, we figured the airplane first flew on an actual power output of 4 hp.

Our next experiment in trying to develop a low cost engine for the "Skeeto" was a chain saw engine (Engine installation # 4) manufactured by "Homelite," and rated at 7½ hp at about 5700 rpm (weight about 20 lbs). Since it was necessary to reduce the speed of the prop, we used a Gilmor timing belt and at low rpms (anything below half throttle) there was a terrific backlash, due to the engine carrying the prop half a revolution and then the prop carrying the engine the balance of the revolution. The timing belts are reinforced with steel and are not supposed to stretch, but this one actually stretched after a 10 minute beating.

In all fairness to the manufacturers of the timing belts, I would like to say that their engineer whom I consulted about using timing belts, recommended that they not be used due to intermittent loads that would be imposed on them, and he was right. I found that a V-belt, although having up to 20% hp loss, (compared to the timing belts 2% to 4% loss), has a good fault in the fact that it can slip and absorb intermittent loads without destruction.

After getting the "Homelite" chain saw broken in, tuned-up and ready to go, I taxied to the end of the runway and opened the throttle. At first the acceleration was amazing, and the tail raised off the ground in less than 100 ft., but about the time I was ready to come back on the stick to break ground, the engine began to slow down, and within another 300 ft., it had frozen tight. On analyzing the trouble, we determined that there wasn't enough cooling air from the normal prop blast to keep this souped-up little 2-cycle cool, and we would have to install a separate blower with baffling to do the job.

Since "Homelite" has no intentions of working with anyone intent on using their engines for anything but what they were manufactured for, we decided to look elsewhere for a suitable engine installation.

Next we installed a 2-cycle, 2-cylinder, in-line engine from an old two-man Disston chain saw, rated at about 9 hp at its best. On the original installation of this engine, it was mounted with the cylinders upright and the prop mounted direct. The direct drive prop loaded the engine down too much and it overheated so badly that all the old type leather seals started leaking, and on the take-off run it would "poop out" and then hardly make it back to the hangar (Engine installation # 5).

In an effort to whip the heating problems and experiment for more prop efficiency with engine, we mounted it inverted and reduced the prop speed 50% using a Gilmor timing belt, and the same prop that we had used mounted direct to the engine. (Engine installation # 6). With this installation, it was necessary to put the flywheel back on the engine because of the backlash. There was quite a bit of "whipping" of the belt which would be very destructive.

On test trials, this installation peaked out at about 4500 rpm, but at this speed, the small flat prop we were using was not turning fast enough to develop the required thrust for take-off. If we had let Carlson whittle out another prop with more "bite" it would have undoubtedly proved satisfactory but not desirable, due to the fact that the engine was not in production and there was no use spending time developing an obsolete engine installation which could not be duplicated in the kits. (Wayne Carlson whittled out a total of seven props for us, free of charge.)

Our next experiment in a power plant was a 25 hp Evinrude outboard engine (Engine installation # 7) which is the same as Johnson and about 3 other well known brands. It was at this time, due to the planned installation of the heavier outboard engine, that we extended the wing tips 3 ft., making the span 30 ft., total wing area 150 sq. ft., and keeping the wing loading with gross weight about 3.1 lbs. per sq. ft.

The outboard engine was originally mounted with the cylinders inverted and a Chevrolet carburetor on the top, or crankcase side, with the prop mounted direct to the flywheel with four ¼" bolts screwed into nuts countersunk into the innerside of the flywheel. The hex flywheel nut was replaced with a 1" diameter by 2" long special machined nut so that the prop would have a shaft or centering pin for exact location.

With the carburetor sitting higher than the fuel tank, we ran into fuel feed problems, so I improvised a fuel pump using intermittent pressure from the crankcase to actuate a spring loaded diaphragm pump. This didn't prove too satisfactory because the fuel came out as a foam rather than as a liquid, possibly due to the rapid pulsing of the diaphragm. We decided to turn the engine over and put the carburetor on the bottom to whip the fuel feed problems, and eliminating the airpockets in the water jacket that could not be bled with the cylinders in that position. The engine would heat up and steam in the very short runs we were able to get out of it while experimenting with the fuel problems.

After turning the engine over with the cylinders on the top, (Engine installation # 8) we mounted a side draft automotive carburetor under the engine with a 90 degree adapter. The largest automotive side draft carburetor we could obtain had a 13/16" venturi, which wasn't sufficient, since 2-cycle engines have twice the flow of air through the venturi than a 4-cycle for the same cubic displacement. We eventually went back to the standard outboard carburetor that came with the engine, mounting it also on the 90 degree adapter. It had about a 1-1/8" venturi and a very poor atomizing principle, about like a fly spray.

Using the outboard carburetor the engine would turn about 3400 rpm (estimated 18 hp) for about 60 seconds and then quit momentarily. After exhausting all the theories of the 2-cycle and outboard "experts," and wasting about 2 weeks, I finally cured the problems by drilling the needle valve seat to about 6 drill sizes larger, to allow more fuel to enter the carburetor bowl. Mounting the prop directly on the outboard engine imposed an entirely different load condition than the normal outboard installation, since it is not allowed to reach its peak or most efficient rpm before the load is imposed, and it burned about twice the fuel (about 5 gals. per hr., estimated.)

In order to get the engine to idle and accelerate satisfactorily, we linked a spark control along with the throttle to advance and retard the ignition at the same time with the throttle, about the same as the original outboard set up.

After settling the carburetor and ignition problems with a "compromise," we began to iron out the engine cooling problems which were apparent that time. My first set-up was a "thermal syphon" system which didn't pan out because the ports in the engine were too small, and water couldn't circulate through the engine fast enough to keep it cool. I also removed the heat rise jacket over the exhaust ports, which is designed to raise the temperature of the water before it reaches the head for normal outboard operation. For a radiator, I used a car heater radiator, relocating the ports and installing a pressure cap and neck taken from a standard automotive radiator.

After trying to whip the thermal syphon system problems for a few days, I went to a "condensation" type system by which the water was allowed to boil and rise as steam to the radiator, condense and run back as water in the other port. It turned out that outboard motors are set up too close a tolerance to run at the temperatures allowed by letting the water boil. After about 3 flights down the runway, the internal temperature of the engine would build up to a point where the pistons would freeze and pull metal. It froze 3 times and I had to overhaul it before continuing the experiments. To finally whip the cooling problems I went to a standrad circulating system and installed a Sears-Roebuck washing machine water pump at the back of the engine where the prop drive shaft normally is installed in the spline fitting.

After playing with the project as a "hobby" for about 8 months (Nov. '56 to June '57, averaging about 25 hours per week,) "Skeeto," the answer to the "poor" pilots' prayers, was finally ready to go, and Roy Outcan our F.A.A. inspector, who for the past many years has nervously stood by and sweated out the first test flights of all of my "brain childs" since "Sky Baby," finally consented to let me take it around the pattern. (By this time I had a total of about 2 hours flying time up and down the runway, playing with these different engine installations.)

With the heavier engine installed and the 2-½ gallon fuel tank full (round 5 gallon gas can split down the middle) the airplane was more than a little nose heavy, and in the last minute confusion (trying to convince the inspector that it would stay together,) I forgot to replace the sandbag ballast in the tail which I used to "equalize" the weight and had just taken out to patch a hole that was leaking sand.

The outboard loaded up very easily when idling and it took about half the take-off run to get the engine cleaned up, firing right, and stop "4-cycling," but as usual it lifted off in about 500 ft. The rate-of-climb was impressive at about 200 fpm, which wasn't bad considering the fact that I had the stick almost all the way back, because of nose heaviness, which created a lot of drag. Since the inspector didn't trust the engine in the first place (or the airplane,) they told me he almost fainted when he heard the engine sputter and almost quit quite a bit beyond gliding distance to the runway, and it worried me a little too, so I cut my "final" short to play it safe.

It seems that due to the "high frequency" engine vibration, the carburetor mixture knobs had turned and changed the mixture. The high frequency vibration of a stripped outboard powerhead, running without the benefit of the prop leg sitting in water dampening the vibration, is not a commonly known fact in the boating field and many people will swear that outboards are smooth. But once they fly around the pattern behind one working under load, they will change their minds.

After the initial flight, the airplane was licensed as a "Research & Development" project (we didn't file as "amateur-built") but the inspector asked me to limit the flights to the length of the runway until the dependability of the engine installation had been established. At this point, after successfully completing "phase #1," I made a complete evaluation of the whole project and decided to drop it right there.

To make space in the hangar for the next project, "Skeeto" was donated intact, minus engine, to the Air Museum at Claremont, California, operated by Ed Maloney, and while he had his big "Semi" over here hauling it away, I also donated the "Stits Junior," former World's Smallest Airplane (1948-52) which has been superseded by the now well-known "Sky Baby."

The flight characteristics of "Skeeto" were a little unusual and cannot be compared with anything I have flown before. It was easier to make turns pushing a lot of rudder and filling in with a little aileron, then waiting for the aileron to react, which was a little slow at 25 to 30 mph. The elevators reacted normally with no unusual characteristics other than light feel. With such a light wing loading, there is no sharp break in the stall, just a gentle letdown, giving the sensation you were flying a balloon.

Quite a bit of money was spent trying to locate suitable engines which could be bought at a reasonable price. The outboard motor installation more nearly approached the requirements for an Ultralight power plant than anything available on the commercial market today, but the price of the installation exceeds the cost of a used Continental 65 hp and doesn't have the dependability or near the hp.

During the 3 or 4 months experimenting with the various engine installations, we contacted about every company in the business, and my experience was that generally the larger companies were not interested in having their engines used on anything that could possibly give them bad publicity. They considered the possible sale of as much as 100 special engines a month to be mounted in aircraft, just a "drip in a rain storm" compared to the hundred thousand or so a year production of their standard designs. One company stated that if I would give them an order for 5000 engines they would build it to my specifications, which seemed to be about the trend of their thinking and I can understand their point. It is not good business to invest money developing a special engine for a limited market.

To save the readers the trouble of writing to me later, and asking why I did not try the "Volkswagen" engine, I have a letter of file over 5 years old, and their reply was they do not sanction the use of their engine in anything but their automobile and industrial installations. They authorized no one to use them in aircraft, and definitely would not sell me any for that purpose. The Volkswagen engine is being used by home-builders in some countries, including France, simply because there is nothing else available, not because they think Volkswagen is best.

For those who advocate the use of motorcycle engines, I will quote the price of $300.00 for a new basic engine (Triumph), but then there's the gear reduction necessary because they turn 6000 and up, the ignition system to change over to magneto, vibration, thrust bearings, and a few other little problems. By the time you get through you have the price of a good 65 hp Continental Lycoming or Franklin engine wrapped up in your installation and not half the performance and dependability. Generally the industrial engines, like the little 10 hp twin, built by Onan & Sons, to power their portable Arc Generator, is too heavy and too expensive, weighing about 10 lbs. per hp after it is "stripped," and the price runs around $300.00

Many of the readers of this article may have the impression that the project was all sweat, trouble and disappointment, but to the contrary, it was a lot of fun, educational, and very interesting. There were many highlights in the project that will never be forgotten, like the times when I had to "bailout" and catch the airplane to stop it before it got to the fence or ditch when taxiing down wind with no rudder control (before I installed the steerable tail wheel.) I didn't bother fastening my safety belt in the early "experiments" because it became quite common to bail out at 10 or 15 mph and grab the airplane. Since I weighed more than the airplane I always got it stopped before hitting anything.

Then there was the time we woke the neighborhood at midnight one Saturday night when we first got the "twin" engines tuned-up, somewhat synchronized, and were lifting it off in a light sprinkle, navigating by automobile lights. With those "short stacks" on the 2-cycle engines, one turning 3500 and the other one about 3700, it sounded like a B-36 taking off.

As a summary of the whole Ultralight project, my opinion is that any aircraft with a 3 or 4 lb. wing loading is not practical. With a 10 mph wind blowing it is necessary to walk the airplane out to the runway to play it safe. With a stalling speed of 18 or 20 mph, there isn't much of a margin between flying and landing, when you have gusts up to 15 mph, which is quite frequent in many parts of the country. As a "novelty" and a "hobby," Ultralights are a lot of fun but just not practical.

I was urged by several interested persons, particularly George Hardie, to make a complete report on my findings and experiments in developing the "Skeeto," and I have tried to give the facts as I see them. I hope that my experiences and the

Fig. 2-41. Klaus in his Fledgling hang glider — seed for some ultralights of the early 1980's.

ground I have covered will be of benefit to others interested in doing work along this line."

Klaus Hill – Modern Day Ultralight Pioneer

No ultralight history would be complete without including Klaus. Not enough can possibly be said about the late Klaus Hill, an extremely prolific ultralight designer. He ate, slept, and thought ultralights during all his waking hours, and eventually gave his life in pursuit of the ultimate ultralight.

Klaus began his contributions to the industry with what is now known as the Fledgling, a high performance (11-to-1 glide ratio) foldable, semi-rigid hang glider. It has since evolved into various makes of a powered Fledge. Several of these have even managed to fly across the continental United States (in many hops), establishing some sort of modern day record.

The year 1974 saw the emergence of the Super Floater ultralight glider. Not really a hang glider, it offered rudder and elevator control and an unheard of glide ratio of 14-to-1! It also incorporated some new concepts in ultralight construction, and became the seedling for one of today's popular ultralights, the twin-engined Lazair from Canada, and more recently the Cloudbuster.

Fig. 2-42. Klaus Hill's "Superfloater" spawned some of today's ultralights. Was foot-launched glider with rudder and elevator controls.

Not to be outdistanced by his "power-hungry" contemporaries, Klaus was once again at the forefront of ultralight technology when he introduced his Hummer at Oshkosh 1978. It was a crowd pleaser. While the other ultralights were merely powered hang gliders, the Hummer was a full-blown assault on the minimum airplane concept. Klaus had done it again, but the FAA was soon to have its say—

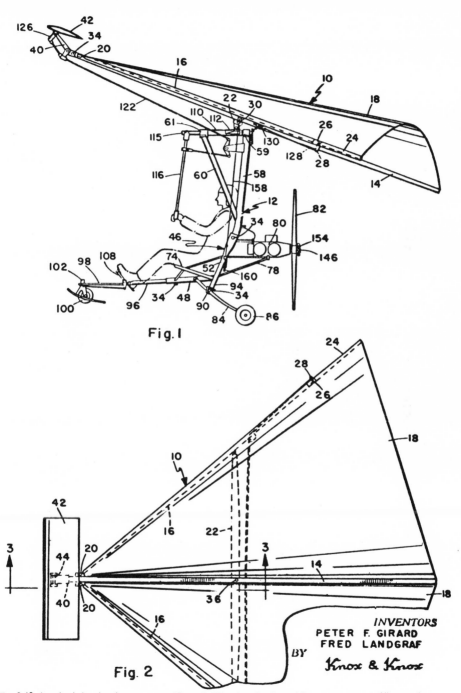

P. F. GIRARD ETAL   3,361,388

DEMOUNTABLE AIRCRAFT WITH FLEXIBLE WING

Filed March 7, 1966   4 Sheets—Sheet 1

Fig. I

Fig. 2

INVENTORS
PETER F. GIRARD
FRED LANDGRAF
BY *Knox & Knox*

Fig. 2-43. A patent drawing for a powered Rogallo Wing foreshadowed the appearance of the modern day "trike".

63

Hummer pilots would be required to possess a student pilot's license because it could not be foot-launched!

Undaunted, and determined to produce a freedom (from licensing and registration) flying machine for non-pilots, Klaus set about the task of designing a foot-launchable version of the Hummer. Appropriately, he called his newest brainchild the Humbug, incorporating some features from the Fledgling hang glider as well as some new thinking. It's the kind of design that is spawning offspring—a classic configuration—like the Hummingbird, Vector 610 and Mirage.

Not everybody could agree with some of Klaus' philosophies, but we can all appreciate his aeronautical genius. He will be sorely missed.

Recent Historical Developments

When the Rogallo flexible wing patent conviently expired in 1968, flight minded enthusiasts around the world siezed the concept for their own. Before too long, sand dunes, ski slopes and other precipitous places became the haven of the hang gliders. Since then, it is estimated that more than a quarter million people have

THE BACK PACK ENGINE

Grab hold of your big toe and hang on tight 'cause here comes the incredible back pack engine. Engineered for safety, performance, and all out fun. Now you can take off, climb, and fly without a slope, cliff, or even wind. Mercy.

vibration free. All you feel is a gentle push on your back. And the twist grip throttle is mounted right up front on the control bar.

So there you go. The back pack engine. A new frontier within a new frontier.

This amazing little unit is powered by a lightweight but husky McCulloch go cart racing engine with tuned exhaust. The three bladed caged propeller develops fantastic thrust, enabling the pilot to lift off even from flat ground. The pack is comfortable and virtually

For more information call or write Bill Bennett, Delta Wing Kite Co., P.O. Box 483, Van Nuys, California 91408 Phone: (213) 785-2474 or 787-6600.

Fig. 2-44. An ad for Bill Bennett's Back Pack Engine was an early 1970's attempt at powered Rogallo flight — didn't catch on.

tasted flight beneath the gossamer wings of a kite, and the sport continues growing. The deceptively simple Rogallo has had a profound impact on the origins of the modern ultralight.

During the early 70's, soon after the advent of the so-called "standard" Rogallo wing hang glider, several flyers began experimenting with power. Notable among the early power pioneers was Bill Bennett. He developed and marketed a unit called the "Back Pack," which was actually strapped to the flyer's back! The powerplant was a 10 hp go-kart engine driving a caged fan. It was to be used with a Rogallo "kite" however, it never really caught on — no doubt due to its weight, vibration, discomfort and marginal performance.

Not long after the appearance of the Rogallo, super lightweight versions of more conventional looking designs were developed as hang gliders. Unlike the kites, which relied solely on "body english" for controls the so-called "rigid wings" featured airplane-like control systems. The Icarus II biplane and VJ-23 Swingwing were two notable early examples. True, they were heavier, more complicated in construction and harder to handle on the ground, but they also offered vastly improved performance, stability and control. While the best Rogallos couldn't exceed glide ratios of nine, the rigids were getting into the high teens. The problem with rigids, as far as most hang glider enthusiasts were concerned, was that they required too much time to build and were too much of a hassel to transport to and up the flying site. Most hard core enthusiasts were interested in flying, not carpentry and metalwork and hauling.

In spite of their poor popularity when originally introduced, non-Rogallo designs continued to develop through the 70's, serving to bring more pilots and professional types into the sport. The airplane-like appearance and control systems instilled a greater degree of confidence about their airworthiness.

At one time, it was thought that hang gliding would become one of the biggest sports in the nation, and while it drew tremendous media attention in the early years, it just wasn't to be. As pure and beautiful a flight form as hang gliding is, it

Fig. 2-45. John Moody foot-launched his way into powered ultralight history after mounting a go-kart engine to his Icarus II hang glider in 1975.

nonetheless is possessed of self-limiting growth factors. First of all, it necessitates the use of vertical terrain with a wind prevailing on its face—needless to say, most of the world is not so endowed. Secondly, the enthusiast must be possessed of a certain degree of physical prowess, not to mention the running with almost reckless abandon down a slope or, worse yet, off a cliff— in order to properly committ aviation.

Suffice it to say, most people are just not all that athletic and/or daring, and don't have mountainous backyards. Furthermore, most folks prefer recreation that does not require much work—the object is to relax and enjoy.

To alleviate the problems inherent in hang gliding, one frustrated flatland flyer (John Moody) got the brilliant idea of mounting a go-kart engine to his Icarus II hang glider in 1975. Originally, the engine was intended to be used as a replacement for vertical terrain—power up, shut-down and soar. The engine was to be used only for climbing. After mountain lift or a thermal was located, the engine could be turned off. If the lift ran out, the engine was there to eliminate an off-field landing in some remote area.

In theory, this all sounded good, while in actuality having a throttle in hand gave the pilot a new sense of freedom. He could now go wherever he wanted to. He was not limited to areas of natural lift. Indeed, ultralights have climbed to over 21,000 feet and covered transcontinental distances while under power.

Some other interesting developments occurred in 1977, when several bolt-on power units were made available for Rogallo hang gliders. One unit consisted of a go-kart engine mounted above the pilot, connected to a shaft driven propeller located at the rear end of the keel. Another featured two chainsaw engines with direct driven props, mounted from the control bar. Curiously, the engine support

Fig. 2-46. Another mid-1970's approach to powered Rogallo flight featured twin engines.

tubes served as gas tanks. The bolt-on power packages allowed the Rogalloist to continue foot-launching while eliminating the need for a mountain. They served as a transition to the currently manufactured "trikes" — a pyramidal structure with engine, seat and landing gear — which bolt to structurally reinforced Rogallo wing hang gliders.

Fig. 2-47. The Volmer VJ-23E foot-launched powered ultralight was the first to cross the English Channel in 1978.

Today, there are more than fifty manufacturers of ultralights, making it the fastest growing segment of the aerospace industry. In 1982 alone, close to 14,000 units were sold—more than double the number of general aviation aircraft made. In fact, most manufacturers report they can't keep up with the demand.

In an effort to insure safety to the consumer and be self-regulating to the point where the FAA has minimal involvement, the ultralight manufacturers have joined together and formed their own organization. Called the PUMA (Powered Ultralight Manufacturers Association), its goal is to provide a unified voice and set standards, including: a flight manual, training program, structural and aerodynamic tests, and dealer criteria.

Section Two
ULTRALIGHT
AERODYNAMICS

Chapter Three

The Atmosphere-
Medium of Flight

Introduction

Flight is amazing, and the more you understand it, the more fascinating it seems to become. Indeed less than a century ago most of the world, including eminent scientists, thought human flight was impossible. Even though birds were looked up at with envy since the beginning of mankind, it wasn't until the invention of the wing (which incidentally, is as basic as the wheel!) that man could hope to fly aerodynamically.

Man's primal urge to overcome gravity by emulating the birds has produced untold weird and wonderful flying machines. Since the "secret" was discovered and man learned the basics of how to fly, he has continually strived to improve his aerial creations. By studying aerodynamics—the science of objects in relative motion with the air—anyone can gain a better understanding of what flight is all about, and be a safer pilot for it.

The modern day aerial recreational adventurer should know as much as possible about the air which makes his flying possible in the first place. Needless to say, without air we couldn't live let alone fly. The air is unlike any other medium on earth and it requires serious study by all who venture aloft. It is a very unforgiving medium and we must play by its rules to insure safe passage. You can't cheat and live to tell about it—at least not for very long. When in Rome, do as the Romans do. When in the air, do as the birds do.

What Is Flight?

The ancient Chinese fired the first missles about 1400 and the French "flew" the first hot air balloon in 1783 but, these devices "flew" only in the broadest sense of the word. A missile does not rely on the atmosphere for its support—it "flies" on a trajectory. After it is launched, its momentum is continually diminished by air resistance and its path arched by gravity as it is gradually pulled toward the earth. Even if a missile is powered while in flight, it'll still return to earth because of gravitational attraction, although it'll "fly" a flatter arc. Only when the missle is accelerated to 17,000 mph can it leave the influence of earth's gravity. While in orbit, it is essentially travelling at such a rate that its centripetal force equals the gravitational pull. If launched in the vacuum of outer space and away from the gravitational influence of a celestial body, a missile would continue on indefinitely due to the lack of air resistance.

A hot air balloon "flys" by the act of displacing a volume of air equal to its weight, much as a boat floats in the water. Since air weighs .075 pounds per cubic foot, a balloon displacing 1000 cubic feet would float if it weighed less than 75 pounds. The problem with balloons is that they are at the mercy of the wind—they just drift with it. A blimp offers some improvement, but it must be large to lift a reasonable payload, and therefore is quite cumbersome. For instance, a cubic foot of helium lifts only an ounce.

Balloons and missiles do not fly. Aerodynamic flight is really what we mean by the word fly, and it is solely dependent upon the movement of surfaces through the air and the reactions generated by their interaction. Aircraft, model aircraft, insects, birds and winged mammals are the only things that fly in the true sense of the word. Before we can understand how flight is achieved we must first consider the atmosphere, its properties and behavior.

The Extent of the Atmosphere

The gaseous mixture that surrounds the earth, known as the atmosphere, comprises but a millionth of the weight of the entire planet. Yet without it the earth as we know it would not exist. A good way to think of the atmosphere is as "an ocean of air in which we are bottom dwellers." It is the only continuous medium through which we can travel anywhere and everywhere. The atmosphere might be called the ultimate "highway," requiring no maintenance or repair.

Since air is a gas it is free to expand in all directions indefinitely, making it almost impossible to give the exact height at which it ends. We can, however, get a good picture of its extent when we consider that half of the total mass of the atmosphere lies below 18,000 feet. Furthermore, if the atmosphere were of uniform density, it would reach only to 26,000 feet. Interestingly, the highest altitude ever attained in a powered, manned aircraft was accomplished by the X-15 rocketplane at 354,00 feet.

Structurally, the atmosphere is considered to consist of six primary "spheres":

the troposphere, stratosphere, mesophere, thermosphere, exosphere, and ionosphere. The troposphere is nearest the earth, and extends to about 30,000 feet at the poles and 60,000 feet at the equator. It is characterized by a decrease in temperature with height of about 3½ degrees Fahrenheit per thousand feet (the lapse rate), until it stops dropping off at the tropopause where the jet stream lies. The troposphere is where most weather occurs and, needless to say, ultralight flight takes place in lower extremeties.

The stratosphere extends from the tropopause (top of the troposphere) up to about 30 miles. It is characterized by a constant temperature of -69.7 degrees Fahrenheit up to about 16 miles, rising from there to about 30 degrees Fahrenheit at 30 miles, where it ends at the stratopause. This temperature rise is caused by ozone, due to its ability to absorb shortwave radiation. The stratosphere is meteorlogically "quiet," offering practically no weather—it is most always sunny and clear.

Above the stable stratosphere, lies the turbulent mesophere where the temperature takes a rapid fall, reaching a minimum near 50 miles, to -134.5 degrees Fahrenheit. Above this, the temperature starts rising again, with altitude, in what is called the thermosphere. Here we see the aurora borealis (northern lights) as well as meteor trails, because there are enough air molecules causing friction to heat the meteor.

A transition zone from atmosphere to outer space exists in a region called the exosphere, extending from 350 to perhaps 1000 miles. Owing to the extremely high temperatures, some air molecules move rapidly enough to escape the earth's gravity and go off into space.

The ionosphere, which extends roughly from 45 to 300 miles, is a zone where ultraviolet radiation dissociates electrons from neutral air molecules and atoms, forming free electrons and positively charged ions. It has important benefits for long range radio communications.

PROPERTIES AND CHARACTERISTICS

As we learned in school, air is a colorless, tasteless, odorless mixture of various elemental gases. What they didn't tell us is that it also contains a host of pollutants, as well. Now let's take a closer look to see what the atmosphere is composed of.

Color and Transparency

Air may be colorless but it does, in fact, present a small degree of blockage to both light and vision. This is especially true near metropolitan areas where pollutants are often suspended in the form of smog. In general though, it is easier to see objects vertically, than horizontally, because of the atmosphere's decreasing density with altitude. The sky looks blue because air molecules are smaller than the wavelengths of blue light (the shortest in the spectrum) and therefore they scatter the blue. The higher you go the thinner the air and the more separated the air molecules become, leading to a darkening of the sky, until it is actually black in space. For particles larger than light waves, the light is scattered all over the spectrum, giving a whitish appearance such as we see in clouds and fog.

Chemical Composition

The air we breathe consists chiefly of about 21% oxygen, 78% nitrogen, and trace amounts of eight other gases. These gases are in a simple mechanical mixture, not chemically combined, and remain practically constant up to about 60,000 feet.

Among the more evident of the minor gasses we find argon, helium, krypton and neon. Carbon dioxide, which is used by plants in photosynthesis and exhaled by animals, reaches a higher percentage in the city than in the country. Ozone, which is an air molecule with an extra oxygen atom attached, varies from almost none in the city to traces in the country, and is formed around electrical discharges such as lightning. Most ozone lies between ten and twenty-five miles and is important in absorbing ultraviolet rays.

Air also holds anywhere from zero to ½% water vapor which mixes just like the other gases, except when it precipitates. Pollutants too, are carried by the air and are especially noticeable around metropolitan areas. Concentrations can be so great that the horizon takes on a reddish brown tint, which when coupled with high relative humidity, can make visibility very poor.

Compressibility

Gases and liquids are both fluids but air, being a gas, has the quality of compressibility, while liquids don't. Under normal circumstances, the volume of a given mass of air is directly proportional to the static pressure acting on it. Doubling the pressure halves the volume, thereby doubling the density as well. Whenever air is compressed, the energy used in doing the compression appears in the air as a temperature rise. Remember how your bicycle tire pump hose heated up when you filled the tires? Conversely, whenever a given volume of air expands, its temperature drops.

Temperature Effects

Heating a volume of air causes it to expand if free to do so, or to increase in pressure if confined within a container. Conversely, cooling a parcel of air reduces its volume, or lowers its pressure if confined within a container.

Changes of State

Like other forms of matter, air can exist as a solid, a liquid or a gas. Air will become a liquid at 220 degrees Fahrenheit while under a pressure of 574 psi. It will solidify when subjected to still greater pressure and lower temperature. Liquid oxygen (LOX) is used as the oxidizer in liquid fueled rockets, while liquid hydrogen is the fuel. LOX, of course, vaporizes under normal atmospheric pressure, looking like steam coming off the rocket.

Pressure

Everyone can relate to the increasing pressure felt as you descend in a swimming pool. The same is true for the atmosphere, except being at sea level, we are already about as deep as we can go and are therefore under its maximum pressure. With perhaps 750 miles of air above us, the pressure exerted on a square inch at sea level is 14.7 pounds per square inch, or 2116.8 pounds per square foot. The higher you go in the atmosphere, the less the pressure. If you were to ascend into the stratosphere without being in a pressurized aircraft or flight suit, you would literally explode because internally your body is at sea level pressure, which is much higher.

In the study of aerodynamics, pressure is normally understood to be the ambient "static" pressure of the atmosphere.

Density

Density is defined as weight per unit volume. Since air can be compressed, its density at sea level is greater than at some higher elevation - more air molecules are squeezed into a unit volume. At sea level, air has a density of .0765 lb./cu. ft. under normal conditions, and half that value at about 22,000 feet.

Air density also decreases with increasing temperature, an important consideration in aircraft performance - engine power drops with decreasing density. Humidity too causes the air density to drop, because water vapor weighs only about 60% as much as a dry volume of air. When the relative humidity rises, you can expect a little less performance.

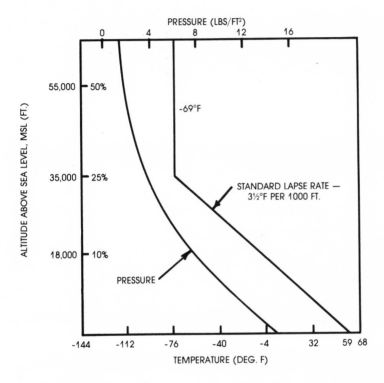

Fig. 3-1. The ICAO Standard Atmosphere. A Standard Day at sea level is 59° and 29.92 inches of mercury.

The Standard Atmosphere

It should be obvious by now that the atmosphere is quite an active place, with conditions varying greatly from place to place and time to time. In order to cope with this situation, aeronautical engineers have devised the so-called "standard atmosphere," giving a base for aircraft performance and design. For instance, if an aircraft is tested at mile high Denver, the performance figures can be "reduced" to the "standard" conditions, so that it can be compared to any other aircraft. Then, too, knowing the performance figures for standard conditions, they can be predicted for any altitude, temperature and humidity.

The standard atmosphere most generally accepted is the ICAO (International Civil Aviation Organization) Standard Atmosphere. It is based on the following assumptions:

75

1. The temperature at sea level is 59 degrees Fahrenheit (15 degrees Celsius).
2. The barometric pressure at sea level is 29.92 in. (760mm) of mercury.
3. The specific weight of such air is 0.07651 lb./cu. ft. at sea level.
4. The specific volume is 13.07 cu. ft./lb. at sea level.
5. The density is 0.002378 slug/cu. ft. at sea level.
6. The temperature gradient, or lapse rate, is 3.566 degrees Fahrenheit/1000 ft. in the troposphere.
7. The temperature is a constant -67 degrees Fahrenheit beginning at 35,332 ft.
8. The air is a perfect dry gas obeying the laws of Charles and Boyle.

Chapter Four

Air In Motion and the Force

THE DYNAMIC PROPERTIES OF AIR

Before we begin our study of aerodynamics, we must become familiar with the dynamic properties of the air itself. When air is set in motion it takes on a new character. Air at rest goes unnoticed, but as soon as it starts to move, we become aware of it. The air's dynamic qualities include: inertia, elasticity, and viscosity.

Inertia

In common with all forms of matter, air has mass, thus weight, and exhibits the phenomenon of inertia. The dictionary defines inertia as: that property of matter by which a mass tends to retain its state of rest or uniform straight line motion unless acted upon by an external force. You may not think of air as having inertia, but consider the Goodyear Blimp and you'll realize that this bag of helium (which is lighter than air) does indeed possess inertia—it takes a good deal of power to move and it cannot be stopped "on a dime." Natural atmospheric phenomenon, such as hurricanes and tornadoes, also demonstrate the air's possession of an awesome inertia. One early aeronautical pioneer expressed it this way, "the air is hard enough if it is hit fast enough."

Elasticity

Elasticity is the one property that distinguishes air and other gases from liquids, which are essentially inelastic. Air and other gases are really the most perfectly elastic substances known; they will withstand tremendous compression for an indefinite period and yet return to their original volume when the pressure is released. Air disturbed by a passing obstruction will return to its original condition after the obstruction has passed.

Viscosity

The dictionary defines viscosity as that property of a fluid which resists change in the shape or arrangement of its elements during flow. In other words, viscosity is fluid friction or "stickiness." For instance, molasses is an extremely viscous fluid, while water is less so and air even less.

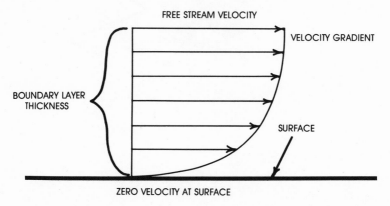

Fig. 4-1. A "boundary layer" forms immediately above the surface over which air flows.

Viscosity reveals its effects whenever a fluid flows relative to a surface. The fluid velocity at the surface is actually zero, rising to the velocity of the object at some distance above its surface. The area of velocity rise is known as the boundary layer, which is normally quite thin, maybe a hundredth of an inch. A "perfect" fluid would not have any viscosity, and the speed of the object would be realized at the object's surface. A good example of the air's viscosity can be demonstrated by driving a dusty car - the dust simply will not blow off, no matter how fast you drive. As air moves over a surface, it tends to stick to it.

It is also important to realize that viscosity, while independent of pressure, increases with decreasing temperature which implies it increases with altitude.

Air In Motion

Whenever air strikes an object, it tends to flow into the area of least pressure and in so doing generates flow patterns so complex they almost defy analysis. While air is compressible, the property does not manifest itself at speeds well below the speed of sound. Since air is practically incompressible at low speeds, the pressure differences produced by an object moving relative to the air make their presence felt some distance in front of the object. This "signals" the air ahead of the object and causes the establishment of a flow pattern in front of the object. Near Mach One, the low intensity pressure waves produced by the object's presence (they radiate at the speed of sound) don't have time to "signal" successive air particles. Consequently, the air piles up, compresses, and forms a shock wave, whenever its velocity reaches the speed of sound.

The Force

As soon as an object begins relative motion with the air, the air around it changes, its dynamic properties arise and a resistance to the desired motion is established. This resistive force is known to all who have walked against a stiff breeze or witnessed the destructive powers of a hurricane. The overwhelming effect of the force is to hinder the motion of objects through the air or to produce pressure on stationary objects. It is a force that man has been aware of since the beginning of his existence, but only in the last hundred years has he learned how to use it to his advantage—to fly.

A simple experiment that anyone can do will demonstrate that the force can be separated into, and recognized to possess, two distinct components. Hold your arm outside the window of a moving car, fingers and thumb together, broadside to the wind, and it wants to blow back. With the hand edgewise to the wind, however, a smaller force is felt in the wind's direction. But rotate the hand upward slightly and the force is up, as well as back. The force in the direction of the wind is called drag, while the force perpendicular to the wind is called lift.

THE FACTORS THAT DETERMINE THE SIZE OF THE FORCE

The magnitude of the force, or pressure, developed by an airstream on an object depends on five primary factors - airspeed, air density, the object's shape, the

AIRFLOW

Fig. 4-2. Streamlines form in the airflow about a streamlined object.

object's area, and the angle between the airstream and the object. The force is also dependent on five secondary factors: the Reynolds Number, and four other items based on the object's aspect ratio (AR), planform, surface roughness, and fineness ratio. Let's examine the effect of these factors on the force.

Airspeed

The force increases as the square of the airspeed. In other words, doubling the airspeed while all other factors remain constant, will quadruple the force.

Air Density

The force decreases in direct proportion to the air density - halving the density means half the weight of air will flow over the object at a given speed, producing half the force. Since air density decreases with altitude, the force will decrease with altitude, all other factors remaining constant.

Area

The force varies directly with the area of the object, provided all other factors remain constant. Doubling the area will double the force because twice the amount of air will be affected by the object's presence.

Shape

Like water, air follows the path of least resistance. More specifically, air always flows from a high pressure region to a low pressure region in the easiest possible path. If an object or outside force is present, the air will be made to alter its course, causing it to generate a force on the object and a flow pattern around it, depending on its shape. The greater the course change, the greater the force. The effect of the object on the airflow pattern can be shown by injecting lines of smoke into the flow. The smoke assumes the path of the streamlines, and shows the relative velocity as well—the closer the lines the faster the flow and the lower the pressure. The further apart the streamlines, the slower the flow and the higher the pressure.

Fig. 4-3. A thin flat plate parallel to the airstream experiences minimal force, all of it in the airflow direction.

A thin, flat plate placed edgewise to an airflow will experience a minimal force, all of it in line with the flow. The streamlines are affected very little by its presence. Positioning the plate broadside to the flow however, will produce a maximum disturbance of the flow. The streamlines separate in front of the plate, accelerate around the edge, then break-up into eddies, forming a turbulent wake and producing a large force parallel to the flow.

If a cylinder is placed around the plate, the force will be lessened—the streamlines in front separate more gradually and aren't as turbulent in the rear. This can be improved even more by tapering the aft end, filling in the turbulent area with the object itself. Still more improvement can be realized by making the circular nose into an ellipse, and giving the aft taper a slight convex curve along with some optimal length or fineness ratio. The top view of a trout shows a high fineness ratio which develops a small force.

Surface Roughness

The finish of the object's surface i.e., its roughness, also plays a part in determining the size of the force developed. It should be apparent that the rougher a surface, the more skin friction will develop between it and the airflow. This is especially true at higher speeds (high RNs), while at lower speeds (low RNs) roughness may actually help. But more on this later. In general, for a body to generate a minimal force parallel to the airstream it must be streamlined. This implies that care must be given in developing the form of the object, with secondary emphasis on its roughness. The lower the airspeed (and RN), the less important roughness becomes, and vice versa.

Angle of Attack

The angle an object makes relative to the airflow is the fifth primary factor in determining the size of the force, and also the most important. As stated

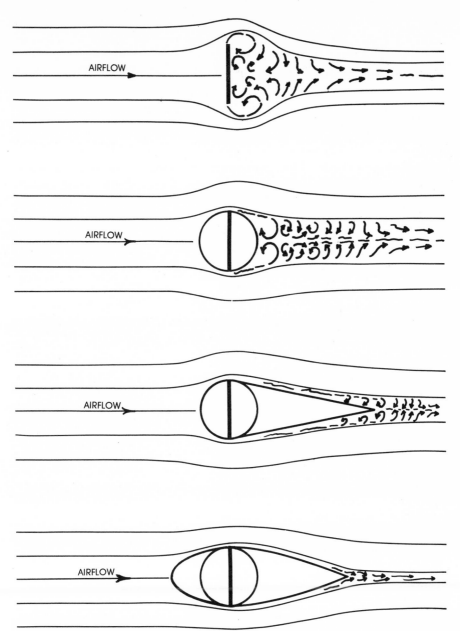

Fig. 4-4. A thin flat plate perpendicular to the airstream will generate a maximum force parallel to the airflow. Streamlining reduces the force.

previously, a flat plate held edgewise to the airflow develops the minimum force possible, but incline it a few degrees and the force increases dramatically *while moving close to being perpendicular to the flow.* In other words, a flat plate inclined slightly to an airflow develops lift, as well as drag, a result of resolving the force into components parallel and perpendicular to the flow, according to the definitions of lift and drag.

Aspect Ratio and Planform

The higher an object's aspect ratio (AR) the more efficient it is as a lifting surface. In other words, long narrow wings produce more lift for a given drag—the force vector is pointed very nearly perpendicular to the relative airflow. A low AR wing, on the other hand, while developing the same lift per area as the high AR wing, has its force vector more rearward than the high AR wing.

The planform of an object, i.e., its shape as viewed from above, is also important to the "quality" of the force produced. As it turns out, the optimal planform is an eliptical shape, which produces the lowest drag for a given lift. But, there are other considerations that enter into the planform selection, which we will leave for a later discussion.

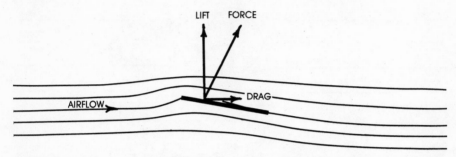

Fig. 4-5. A thin flat plate inclined a few degrees to an airflow generates a large force that is nearer to being perpendicular to the airflow than parallel to it.

Chapter Five

The Boundary Layer

The first physical reality of aerodynamics that we need to understand, is the boundary layer and its characteristics. In a theoretically ideal fluid, it would not exist, but real air has viscosity, which makes it tend to adhere to the surface over which it flows, as well as to itself. At the surface of an object moving relative to the air, the air has no speed. The further out you go from the surface the faster the airspeed, until the free stream velocity is reached at the top of the boundary layer. In other words, the boundary layer is that distance above a surface in which an air velocity gradient exists. Outside the boundary layer, the air is considered non-viscous.

Fortunately, the boundary layer is quite thin, measuring only a small fraction of an inch near a leading edge, to perhaps an inch near the trailing edge. The higher the angle of attack, the larger the boundary layer. Even though the boundary layer is so thin in comparison to an airfoil's thickness, it has a profound affect on an airfoil's characteristics, and must be considered in airfoil design.

The single most important characteristic of a boundary layer is the condition of the flow of the various layers of air particles—laminar or turbulent. A laminar boundary layer is characterized by smoothly flowing layers of air and exhibits a very angular velocity gradient. A turbulent boundary layer, on the other hand, has the various layers of air mixing with each other, while exhibiting a much "fuller"

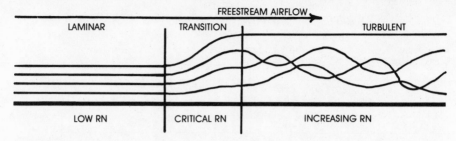

FREESTREAM AIRFLOW

LAMINAR   TRANSITION   TURBULENT

LOW RN   CRITICAL RN   INCREASING RN

Fig. 5-1. The boundary layer over a surface subjected to an airflow starts out laminar, then transitions to a turbulent condition at some "critical" Reynolds Number.

velocity profile—it contains more energy than a laminar boundary layer because of the higher velocity air mixing with the lower, slower layers. The area where a boundary layer changes from laminar to turbulent is known as the transition point.

We can cite a couple of everyday examples to give you a better picture of what goes on in a boundary layer. A lighted cigarette lying in an ashtray in a still room has its smoke rising smoothly and without mixing, for several inches. At some point

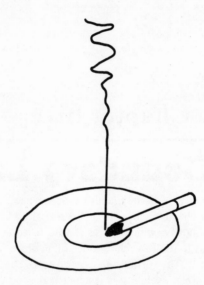

Fig. 5-2. Smoke rising from a cigarette in a still room starts out laminar then transitions to turbulent as it rises.

however, the thin laminar column of smoke breaks up and transitions into a turbulent condition, as it mixes with the room air.

Another common example of laminar and turbulent flows can be demonstrated at the kitchen sink—your faucet. Run the water slowly and you have a nice, glass smooth, laminar column of water. Slowly increase the flow and you'll see "waves" develop within the column—a transition. Increase the flow still more and the water will become turbulent as it mixes with itself and the air. Now try pouring a heavy liquid, such as maple syrup. No matter how fast you try to pour, it comes out laminar—its viscosity is so high that any turbulence, or irregularities in the flow, are damped out.

The Reynold's Number

So how can we determine the condition of the boundary layer? Back in 1883, an English physicist named Osborne Reynolds gave us the answer. By experimenting with fluid flowing in pipes, he developed one of the most important relationships in aerodynamics. His tests led to the development of a dimensionless ratio—the Reynolds Number or RN for short—which is used to determine the state of the boundary layer. This number is simply the ratio of the dynamic forces divided by the viscous forces, which can be expressed mathematically as:

$$RN = pVl/u$$

where:
- p = air density
- V = airspeed
- l = chord length
- u = the coefficient of air viscosity

Luckily, the Reynolds Number of a wing in flight can be given in much simpler terms, since density and viscosity are taken as constants under standard conditions. Therefore

$$RN = 9341 \times Vl$$

where:
- V = airspeed in mph
- l = chord length in feet

A typical ultralight with a chord length of four and a half feet would have a stalling speed (25 mph) Reynolds Number of approximately 1,000,000. At a cruise of 50 mph, the RN would equal 2,000,000.

Some typical values of Reynolds Numbers for various types of aircraft

Aircraft Type	Reynolds Number
C5A Military Transport	100,000,000
Jet Liner	10,000,000 up
Light Aircraft	2,000,000 up
Ultralight	1,000,000 up
Hang Glider	750,000 up
Man-Powered Aircraft	500,000 up
Radio Controlled Model Airplane	300,000 up
Baseball	230,000
Large Soaring Bird (Albatross)	200,000
Seagull	100,000
Small Indoor Model Airplane	10,000
Butterfly gliding	7,000

NOTE: The above figures depend on actual airspeed and wing chord. Boundary layer flows are generally turbulent by RN's of 500,000.

The Reynolds Number is most important when scaled down models of full size aircraft are to be wind tunnel tested. In order to simulate the airflow characteristics of the prototype, a model must be tested at the same RN as the prototype. Fortunately, since the air density and viscosity are constant, all we need do is make the products of the wing chord times velocity equal. If the model is 1/5 full size, it will have to be tested at 5 times the prototype's airspeed. Simulating the RN is important, for lower RN's mean that the lift decreases and the drag increases—the viscosity of the air begins to play a larger role the slower you go and the smaller you get.

Transition

There are two other factors, besides Reynolds Number, that help determine when a flow will transition from laminar to turbulent—surface roughness and the degree of turbulence in the free air. The rougher the surface and/or airstream turbulence, the sooner the boundary layer flow will turn turbulent.

NOTE: It is important to understand that while we base RN on chord length, the RN is in reality growing continuously from zero at the stagnation point to its maximum value at the trailing edge.

Since a laminar flow boundary layer is so smooth, with successive air layers gradually approaching the speed of the free airstream, it stands to reason that it produces less skin friction than a turbulent boundary layer. This would lead us to believe that laminar flow should be the airfoil designer's goal, but it normally isn't! In most instances, turbulent flow is what we're after, for while the skin friction is higher, the momentum of a turbulent boundary layer is better able to cope with surface irregularities such as waviness, crushed insects, etc.

Separation

A turbulent boundary layer is also much better equipped to follow surfaces sloping away from the general airflow, such as the upper surface of an airfoil aft the high point. As air approaches a surface angled toward it, the velocity is continuously increasing while the pressure is decreasing. This is known as a favorable pressure

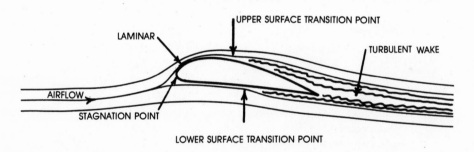

HOW THE BOUNDARY LAYER GROWS WITH DOWNSTREAM POSITION ON AN AIRFOIL.

Fig. 5-3. An unflapped ultralight airfoil will stall at approximately 14 degrees angle of attack, depending on the airfoil and Reynolds Number. When that happens, the boundary layer becomes extremely large and the airflow separates from the upper surface, causing a reduction in lift and an increase in drag.

gradient—the flow is literally pressed onto the surface and follows its contours readily. Once the high point is reached however, the surface slopes away from the airflow, the air decelerates and the pressure begins to rise. This is known as an adverse pressure gradient. It forms an effective barrier, as far as the airflow is concerned, which requires additional energy to be overcome—energy not available in a laminar boundary layer. This lack of energy leads to the flow actually leaving the surface, causing an increase in drag, a decrease in lift and an early stall. The higher the angle of attack, the greater the separation. A turbulent boundary layer allows a much higher angle of attack before total separation and stall. Its extra energy enables the airflow to penetrate the adverse pressure gradient and keep the flow attached for a longer distance.

The Stall

If you don't understand anything else about flying, you *must* understand the stall. It is the single most important characteristic of your airplane; if an airplane is stalled it is not flying. Besides, over half of all aviation deaths are stall related—a most sobering fact.

Aside from the conditions of your airfoil's boundary layer, which you cannot do much about, the stall of any wing is primarily dependent upon the angle of attack. If your wing is below the stall angle of attack, you will not stall. Now, many will say that stall is dependent on airspeed, and it is, but not solely. If we are flying along in straight and level unaccelerated flight, our airplane will stall at a certain airspeed every time. If under additional load, say due to a turn or turbulence, the stalling airspeed increases, but the stall angle of attack does not; it remains constant no matter what the maneuver. Now, there are angle of attack meters available but they're expensive. The best advice, therefore, is to use your airspeed indicator, knowing the stalling speed at various angles of bank, and to carry enough extra speed above stall speed to handle potential stalling in gusts and turns.

There are methods of increasing the lift of an airfoil so it stalls at a higher angle of attack, but more on that later.

Chapter Six

The Theories of Lift

LIFT - THE THEORIES

By definition, lift is the force generated by an object perpendicular to the relative wind—the component of the force on the object normal to the airflow. In straight and level flight, lift is the force that opposes gravity thereby supporting an aircraft. How and why it is generated can be explained in several different ways. Classically, it is recognized to be caused by low pressure on top of the wing and high pressure on the bottom. Theoretically, it can also be explained by the so-called "circulation" theory. And furthermore, it can even be said that it is simply the reaction to the downward deflection of air—in accordance with Newton's Third Law of Motion.

No matter which explanation seems most plausible to you, and we shall examine all three, we can all agree that lift does indeed exist. In fact, evidence of all three theories manifests itself whenever a wing moves relative to the air. Pressure measurements taken around a lifting wing section are lower than static on the upper surface and higher than static on the lower surface. Multiplying the pressure differences by the total wing area yields the lift. Making the streamlines visible and photographing them with the camera stationary with respect to the streamlines, shows a circular flow around the airfoil. And finally, multiplying the velocity of the downwash behind the wing times the area of a circle whose diameter is the wingspan, equals the lifting force.

Bernoulli's Principle

In 1738, a Swiss scientist named Daniel Bernoulli discovered a fundamental law of fluid dynamics. Experimenting with fluids flowing in pipes, he found that whenever the flow velocity increased, the pressure exerted on the pipe walls decreased. The same principle can be used to explain lift.

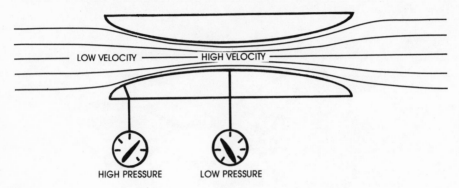

Fig. 6-1. Air flowing through a venturi is forced to speed-up, while the pressure shows a corresponding decrease.

Let's suppose we have a venturi, as shown, with air flowing through it. Taking pressure measurements along the curved wall restricted area we find that the more restricted the area of flow, the faster the velocity and the lower the pressure. Remove the upper half of the venturi and you have a fair airfoil—the pressure over the top decreases as the velocity rises to a maximum near the top.

Bernoulli's principle can be demonstrated quite easily at home. Take a sheet of typing paper and hold a corner with each hand. Curve the front edge down and

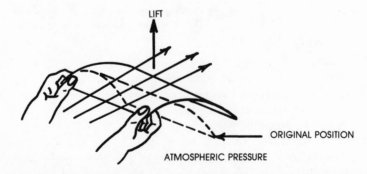

Fig. 6-2. Blowing across a sheet of paper reduces the air pressure above it, causing it to be pushed up by the atmospheric pressure below.

blow across the top of the sheet. The increased air velocity of the air mass over the sheet experiences a reduction in pressure, as compared to the static air under the sheet (which is at 14.7 pounds per square inch), and the sheet rises.

Re-configuring the bottom half of our venturi into a proper airfoil and subjecting it to an airflow, we again measure the pressures along the surface, both upper and lower. We can represent the pressures measured by arrows, as shown. First of all, any object immersed in air experiences atmospheric pressure evenly distributed, all around it (Line 1). When an airfoil begins to move, the pressure distribution

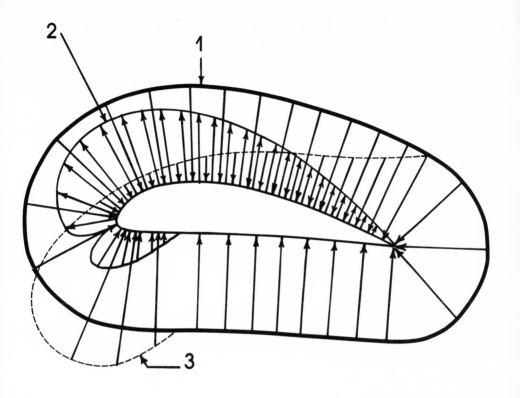

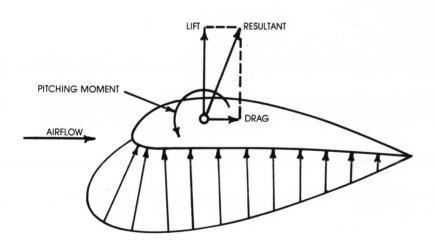

Fig. 6-3. Pressure distribution around a moving airfoil results in lift and drag. Line 1 shows the static pressure that surrounds all things in the atmosphere. Line 2 shows the pressure change generated by the relative airflow. If 2 were taken alone, we'd be inclined to believe a vacuum exists — but that cannot be. Line 3 tells the real story. The pressure on top of the airfoil is less than static, but still positive. Line 3 is simply the addition of lines 1 and 2. If we subtract pressures on both the upper and lower surfaces, we arrive at the net pressure distribution and the resultant force "R". Resolving "R" into components yields lift and drag. We can also see that the pressure distribution gives rise to a nose-down pitching moment.

changes—lower than static over the top, and higher than static on the bottom (Line B). Adding the additional pressure on the bottom and subtracting the reduced pressure on top results in the total pressure on the airfoil in flight (Line C). Notice that the upper surface pressure is still positive and never a vacuum—it just drops below the local atmospheric pressure. Subtracting pressures on opposite sides results in an illustration depicting a net upward force on the airfoil. This can then be represented by the force "F" which is normally resolved into the components of lift and drag.

Understanding Bernoulli's Principle

If an elevated object, such as an airplane, descends, it loses its potential energy (altitude) but converts it into kinetic energy, or forward motion. If your engine fails at altitude, the potential energy available is converted into kinetic energy allowing you to glide to a landing. No energy is destroyed—it is simply converted from one form to another. Note however, that some of the kinetic energy is wasted in the form of drag. The less the drag the further you can glide from a given altitude.

When we talk about airflow and Bernoulli's principle, we are also talking about the conservation of energy within that particular airflow. Air has both pressure energy and kinetic energy—under pressure it possesses the potential to do work on expanding, while under motion it has momentum. The conversion of kinetic energy to potential energy is what Bernoulli's law is all about. As the velocity of an airstream increases (i.e., its kinetic energy increases), its pressure decreases keeping the total energy in the flow at same constant value, depending on velocity and the static pressure.

At this point it is useful to mention what happens when a given mass of air flows through a venturi, or any restricted area. The velocity is inversely proportional to the cross sectional area—halving the area doubles the velocity while decreasing the pressure. This is such an important physical characteristic of airflow that we'll show the mathematical relationship for your reference:

It is easy to see that for the "constant" of our particular airflow to remain constant, whenever the velocity "V" increases the static pressure "P" must decrease. When the velocity becomes zero, such as at the nose of an airfoil (called the stagnation point) the pressure "P" reaches a maximum, since it alone must equal the constant. Interestingly, the pressure at the stagnation point is equal to $\frac{1}{2}\rho V^2$, which is known as the impact or dynamic pressure of the flow.

Circulation Theory Of Lift

It is well known fact that a baseball thrown with a spin will curve, but why? The explanation is quite simple. Since air is viscous it adheres to the spinning baseball, imparting a circulatory component to the flow at the ball's surface. This increases the air velocity on the side rotating with the relative wind, while decreasing the velocity on the side rotating against the relative wind. The result is a pressure difference, or sideways "lift," that causes the ball to curve. This phenomenon is also useful in imparting spin to a tennis ball by "cutting" it causing it to drop, and by "slicing" a golf ball to make it rise.

If an infinitely long cylinder is placed in an airflow and rotated, it will develop lift too, by the same principle as the spinning baseball. This is the key to the circulation theory of lift. Until this was realized, theoretical models of airflow around airfoils always gave the result that lift could not be developed. No wonder

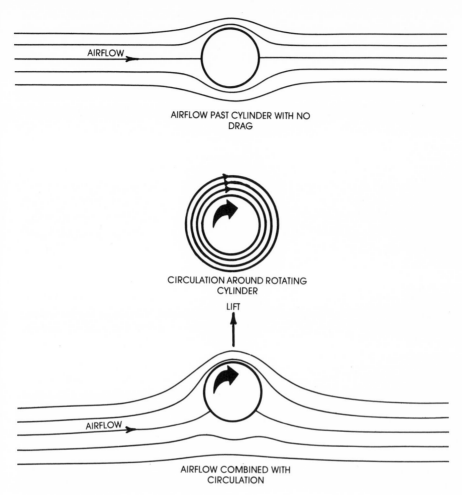

AIRFLOW

AIRFLOW PAST CYLINDER WITH NO
DRAG

CIRCULATION AROUND ROTATING
CYLINDER

LIFT

AIRFLOW

AIRFLOW COMBINED WITH
CIRCULATION

Fig. 6-4. The basis for the "circulation theory of lift."

mathematicians thought flight was impossible. The theories also showed there to be
an infinite airspeed at the trailing edge—clearly an impossibility!

Early in the twentieth century a German mathematician named Wilhelm Kutta
and a Russian professor of mechanics named Nikolai Joukowsky proposed that
"circulation" be added to the theoretical airfoil model to eliminate the impossible
condition at the trailing edge. This superimposed circulation had the effect of
increasing the airspeed over the upper surface, while decreasing it below the lower
surface. The result was lift, with the flow leaving tangent to the trailing edge—the
"Kutta condition." Joukowsky later showed that the lift could be calculated by
multiplying the air density times the airspeed times the circulation factor. This
means that the "circulation" ($\daleth$) is equal to the wing area times the coefficient
of lift divided by two ($\daleth = \frac{1}{2}\ SC_L$). Mathematically the lift due to circulation
equals ρ V.

While the circulation theory may sound unreal, it has been observed to exist.
Due to the viscosity of the air, the frictional forces near an airfoil's surface actually
induce a net circulation around the airfoil. The airflow over the upper surface

93

speeds-up (lowering the pressure) while the airflow below the lower surface slows-down, increasing the pressure. The net result is, of course, lift. The two photos included here are proof. They both show a rotary motion of the streamlines, called a vortex, as they leave the airfoil. The vortices are caused by the presence of the airfoil and the circulation around it. The noted aerodynamicist Theodore von Kármán stated the relationship of vortex motion of the generation of lift concisely in his book *Aerodynamics:* "Now we must remember that, according to a fundamental principle of mechanics, a rotation, or more exactly a moment of momentum, cannot be created in a system without reaction. For example, if we try to put into rotation a body, such as a wheel, we experience a reaction to rotate

EQUAL AND OPPOSITE CIRCULATION

STARTING VORTEX

Fig. 6-5. The faster airflow over the upper surface and slower airflow under the bottom surface gives rise to a net circulation around the airfoil, which is equal but opposite to the starting vortex.

us in the opposite direction. Or in the case of a helicopter with one rotor turning in one direction, we need a device to prevent the body of the craft being put into rotation in the opposite sense. Similarly, if the process of putting a wing section in motion creates a vortex, i.e., a rotation of a part of the fluid, a rotation in the opposite sense is created in the rest of the fluid. The rotary motion of the fluid appears as the circulation around the wing section."

The Momentum Theory of Lift—Downward Deflection of Air

The momentum theory of lift is perhaps the easiest of all to understand. It is based solely on Newton's Second and Third Laws of Motion which state that: force is equal to mass times acceleration, and for every action there is an equal but opposite reaction. With this theory we don't care about the details of pressure differences or circulations. All we are concerned with are the gross effects of the airfoil on the airflow.

The momentum theory of lift assumes that a wing serves simply as a device which deflects air downward, and reacts by developing lift. Applying Newton's Second Law of Motion, we find that a net force is developed on the wing equal to the mass of air deflected per unit time, times the change in its vertical velocity. Assuming the air affected by the passage of a wing is equal to an ellipse with its major axis equal to the wing span, and its minor axis about 88% of the major axis, we can actually calculate the lift. Multiplying the area of the ellipse times the air density times the airspeed gives us the mass flow rate of the air affected by the wing. To find the lift force, all we need do is multiply the mass flow rate times the airspeed times the angle of downwash. In other words, lift is equal to the downward momentum of the air deflected in a unit of time.

In all three theories of lift, no criteria were listed regarding the specific shape of the airfoil. As mentioned previously, a flat plate inclined to an airflow is all that is

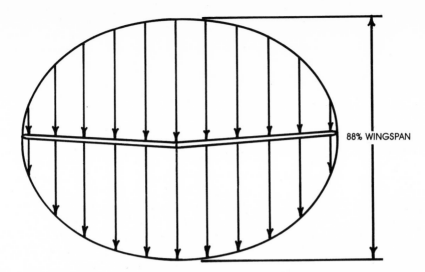

Fig. 6-6. The area affected by a lifting wing is an ellipse with minor axis equal to 88% of the wing span.

necessary to generate lift. In fact, the increase in lift with angle of attack, i.e., the slope of the lift curve, is the same for flat plates as it is for proper airfoils. However, flat plates are not used for wings because they can develop only low lift and a very abrupt stall.

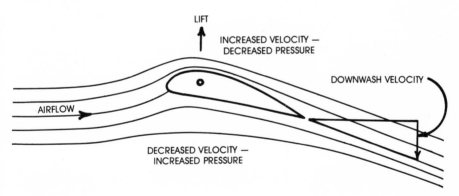

Fig. 6-7. Lift is the reaction of the airfoil to deflecting the elliptical cross-section of air at a particular downwash velocity.

Lift—The Big Picture

So how can the generation of lift best be explained? Does it matter anyway?

If we look at the "big picture" we see that all three theories are in evidence—you can't have one without the other two. Bernoulli's principle is supported by the existence of increased velocity and decreased pressure on the upper surface, while the lower surface experiences decreased velocity and increased pressure. The circulation theory can also explain the pressure differentials and shows further evidence when photographs of visible streamlines are taken. Finally, the momentum theory manifests itself through the existence of downwash. So we see that lift involves all three.

The theory of lift is a little like the proverbial chicken and the egg—which came first doesn't really matter because all are present! An airfoil cannot deflect air

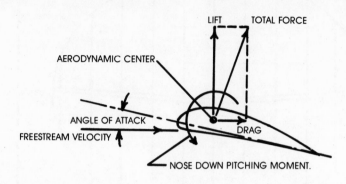

Fig. 6-8. The forces on a lifting airfoil.

downward without giving rise to a pressure differential between its upper and lower surfaces. Conversely, a pressure difference between the upper and lower surfaces of an airfoil results in a downward deflection of air. And furthermore, a downward deflection of air and a pressure differential gives rise to a system of vortices aft of the wing, which must be counterbalanced by a net circulation about the airfoil. Therefore, when we talk about the generation of lift, we can use any and all of the theories to explain it and be totally correct.

Now that we have the theoretical concepts under our belts, let's take a look at the more practical aspects of aerodynamics.

Chapter Seven

Drag-the Force that Holds Airplanes Back

By definition, drag is the force generated by an object parallel to the relative wind—it's the component of the force acting on the object in the direction of the airflow. In straight and level flight it is overcome by the thrust of the propeller. The goal of all aircraft designers is to minimize drag, so as to improve performance, while minimizing power and fuel requirements. Normally what looks good aesthetically, is superior aerodynamically. The reduction of drag, however, is not an easy task and it's perhaps the designer's most challenging chore.

Drag is generated by every part of an aircraft exposed to the airstream. For analysis, it can be broken down into two basic types, induced and parasite—the latter being made up of several components: skin friction drag, form drag, profile drag, interference drag, trim drag, control drag, and cooling drag.

induced drag The energy consumed by the trailing vortex system downstream of a three dimensional wing, is a by product of the generation of lift. But, more on wings later. An airfoil cannot develop induced drag because it is two-dimensional, i.e., it has no span.

parasite drag All the drag not associated with the generation of lift, i.e., all drag but induced drag.

Now let us take a look at the various components of parasite drag.

Skin Friction Drag

Whenever air flows over a surface, it is slowed down in the boundary layer by the tangential shearing forces generated between the air and the surface. The skin friction drag generated is directly proportional to the wetted (surface) area, and also to the square of the velocity, depending on the surface roughness. Generally, if the surface roughness is within the thickness of the boundary layer, there is little effect on the skin friction drag. If the roughness is nearly as high as the boundary layer however, any laminar flow that may have existed will be caused to turn turbulent.

For a thin flat plate at Reynolds Numbers below 100,000, the boundary layer is essentially laminar and the coefficient of skin friction drag, C_f, is as low as it can be. At 100,000 though, the flow generally turns turbulent and the C_f jumps up into another relationship with Reynolds Number. Most surfaces on an ultralight are under turbulent boundary layer conditions, except perhaps for cables and struts.

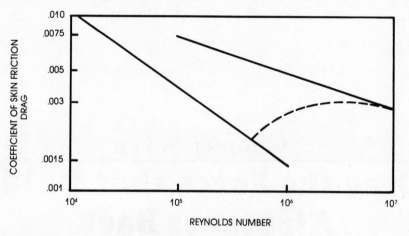

Fig. 7-1. How thin flat plate skin friction drag varies with Reynolds Number.

Form Drag

The shape, or form, of an object is of primary importance in the reduction of drag. The form drag is due to the pressure difference existing from in front of to behind an object. A flat plate perpendicular to an airflow is a good example of the most severe case of form drag—all the drag generated is due to the pressure difference between the positive upstream and negative downstream sides. There's no surface for the air to flow over to generate any skin friction drag.

Form drag is also dependent on Reynolds Number. To illustrate this, let's consider a circular cylinder. For low Reynolds Numbers (under 100,000) the flow is laminar. At the nose, or stagnation point, the static pressure is highest, while being minimal at the cylinder's top and bottom. Beyond the center, the pressure starts rising again, but the laminar boundary layer doesn't have enough momentum to "plow through" this increased pressure. Therefore, the flow separates from the cylinder's surface slightly aft the center, leaving a large turbulent wake and a high form drag.

For higher Reynolds Numbers (above 500,000) the boundary layer turns

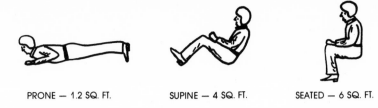

PRONE — 1.2 SQ. FT.   SUPINE — 4 SQ. FT.   SEATED — 6 SQ. FT.

Fig. 7-2. Relative drag of a man in various positions.

turbulent before reaching the laminar separation point, adding to the flow's momentum. This extra energy allows the flow to remain attached for a longer distance with a reduced wake and less form drag as a result. Even though the skin friction drag is higher due to the turbulent boundary layer, the overall drag of the higher Reynolds number case is less than in the laminar case because of the reduced form drag. This is a most important observation for it tells us that, paradoxically, turbulent boundary layer flows are generally desirable.

Now, let's suppose we have a cylinder with a low Reynolds Number separated flow for which we'd like to reduce the drag. What to do? Well, believe it or not, we

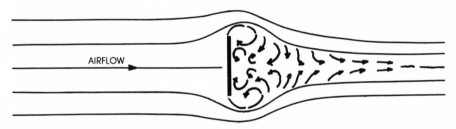

AIRFLOW

Fig. 7-3. The drag of a thin flat plate normal to the airflow is practically all form drag.

must add roughness. By gluing strips of sandpaper to the front half of the cylinder, we will force the otherwise laminar boundary layer flow to go turbulent, thereby energizing it with more momentum. The result is a smaller wake and reduced drag. Competition type model airplanes often employ this technique known as "tripping the boundary layer." Sometimes, a small wire is actually mounted above the wing leading edge to accomplish this.

For unstreamlined bodies, the trailing edge shape is more important than the leading edge, in regards to drag. For instance, assume we have a man sitting out in the airstream, as in many ultralights. That man offers a lot of form drag and turbulence. The most important reduction in that drag can be realized by placing a tapered afterbody *behind* the pilot. This afterbody fills the low pressure wake region, allowing the air to flow more smoothly aft the pilot. The improved airflow, in turn, minimizes the turbulence at the tail and probably allows greater control authority.

Profile Drag

Profile drag is defined as the sum of the skin friction and form drag of various streamlined shapes. It is normally associated with airfoils (as two-dimensional objects,) but also applies to three-dimensional bodies, such as: fuselages, pods, nacells and external fuel tanks. At some optimum fineness ratio (length divided by maximum thickness) the minimum profile drag will exist. At low fineness ratios form drag predominates, while skin friction drag grows with increasing fineness

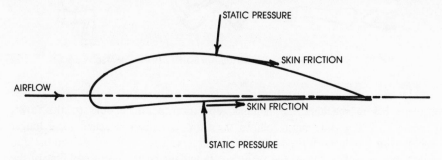

Fig. 7-4. A streamlined body has both form drag and skin friction drag.

ratios, due to the greater surface area.

Several illustrations are presented to show how the drag coefficient varies with body fineness ratio, airfoil thickness ratio and Reynolds number. As shown, the 2-D and 3-D drag coefficients are equal at a fineness of 4, rising sharply as they approach 1, but very gradually above fineness values of 2 (for the sphere) and 4 (for the cylinder.) This would suggest that fineness ratios on the order of 3 or 4 be used to be on the safe (low) drag side. Indeed, non-lifting wing struts are normally designed with a cross section fineness of around 3 or 4.

Airfoils and struts in thickness ranges from 0% to 20% show a profile drag coefficient that varies practically linearly with thickness. The thinner the airfoil (the higher its fineness) the smaller its profile drag. However, we cannot use

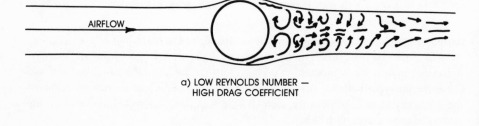

a) LOW REYNOLDS NUMBER —
HIGH DRAG COEFFICIENT

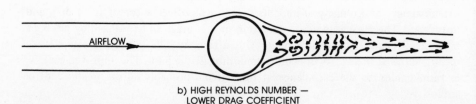

b) HIGH REYNOLDS NUMBER —
LOWER DRAG COEFFICIENT

Fig. 7-5. How the wake aft a circular cylinder changes with Reynolds Number. a) This is a case of separation of a laminar boundary layer. b) Here we have separation delayed because the boundary layer turned turbulent, allowing the flow to remain attached longer.

thinness alone in designing a good airfoil, for other factors take precedence - but more on that later. Above 20% thickness however, the profile drag coefficient increases more rapidly due to separated flow and the build up of pressure (form) drag.

Besides frontal or surface area, it is useful to compare the profile drag coefficient of various streamlined objects, based on their volume. This is particularly important when considering engine nacelles, pilot pods, fuselages and fuel tanks. Fortunately, the coefficient of drag based on volume varies little with fineness ratio, in fact, it is minimal around a fineness of 6, and grows slowly thereafter.

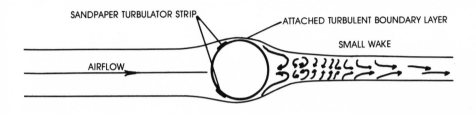

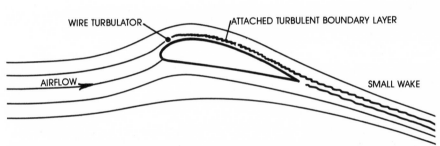

Fig. 7-6. Low Reynolds Number laminar flow can be forced to go turbulent by applying various roughness forms to the leading edge of an object, thereby reducing the overall drag.

A good example of minimizing profile drag and the compromise necessary between skin friction and form drag is the golf ball. In the early days, smooth golf balls were used. As they got used and roughed-up, they seemed to fly further—and they did. The dimpled golf ball of today is the result. While the old smooth balls had laminar boundary layer flow, they suffered an early separation and a high profile drag. The modern balls have a turbulent boundary layer and higher skin friction, but the flow remains attached for a longer distance resulting is less form drag and less profile drag.

To minimize an ultralight's profile drag, a good compromise is required between laminar and turbulent boundary layers. In general though, laminar flow can be expected back to about 35% chord on clean wings. For wire braced, sailcloth covered wings however, the existence of much laminar flow is doubtful.

At any rate, the importance of streamlining cannot be overstated, with minimizing form drag high on the list of priorities. A dramatic example of the value of streamlining in basic turbulent boundary layer flow is that the drag of a 3/32" coated cable is about 7½ times as high as the drag of the same thickness streamlined body of fineness ratio 4. In other words, for the same drag that a lowly cable

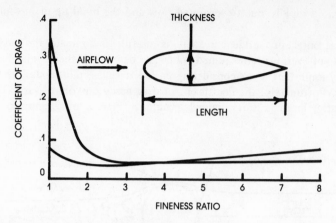

Fig. 7-7. How drag coefficients vary with fineness ratio for two and three dimensional streamlined shapes.

offers, you could move a strut 7½ times as thick through the air at the same airspeed and power!

Interference Drag

Whenever two bodies operate close to each other or intersect, the total drag created is greater than the sum of the drags of the bodies alone! Wherever a wing meets a fuselage, a vertical tail intersects a horizontal tail, an engine mounts to a wing, a strut ties into a wing, a cable joins a tube, etc., interference drag is

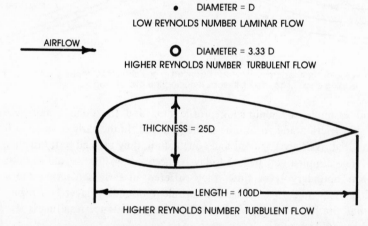

Fig. 7-8. These two-dimensional shapes offer the same coefficient of drag! Above Reynolds Numbers high enough to produce a turbulent boundary layer, the streamlined section can be 7½ times as thick as the circular cylinder (e.g., bracing cable) in similar flow, and as much as 25 times as thick as the circular cylinder in laminar flow.

created. Interference drag is so difficult to estimate, that aeronautical engineers simply add from 5% to 10% of the sum of the individual component drags to allow for it. One reason biplanes are aerodynamically inferior is due to the interference drag generated between the wings.

One instance where interference drag is favorable occurs when race car drivers practice the technique of "drafting." Here, the following car operates in the

102

forward car's wake, which offers a low pressure region of essentially "dead" air. If the following car is close enough to the leader, his drag can actually become negative—he is literally "sucked" along.

Other Forms of Parasite Drag

trim drag Drag created by the aerodynamic forces needed to trim an aircraft to fly at a certain airspeed or glide path. It normally comes from adjusting the horizontal tail and appears as additional induced and form drag. In a flying wing, such as the Mitchell B-10 and U-2, trim drag is generated by the stabilators.

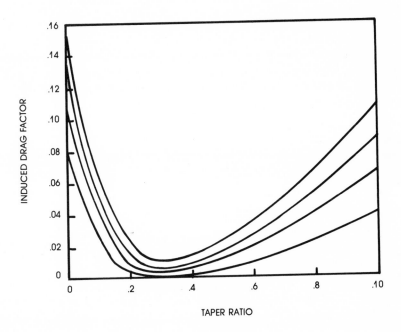

Fig. 7-9. How induced drag varies with taper ratio and aspect ratio.

control drag Additional drag created by the deflection of control surfaces, such as occurs during maneuvers. Improperly designed control surfaces and/or poorly sealed control surface gaps generate unnecessary added induced and form drag.

cooling drag Drag caused by the passage of air over and through the powerplant installation, as required for proper cooling in the form of profile and form drag.

Induced Drag

Parasite drag is quite obvious and readily understood—expose an object to an airstream and it generates parasite drag. But induced drag is something else—it is developed only when that object generates lift. To understand induced drag we must look at the wing as a real, three dimensional body. Airfoils (which are two dimensional) cannot experience induced drag. Where the parasite drag coefficient is nearly constant and equal to the total drag of an aircraft at zero lift, the induced drag coefficient increases with the square of the lift coefficient. And, since the lift coefficient increases as airspeed decreases, the induced drag rises for slower speeds. Half the airspeed means four times the lift coefficient and sixteen times the induced drag.

Induced drag is also dependent upon the aspect ratio of the lifting surface, or wing. The higher the aspect ratio, the more efficient the wing and the lower the induced drag it generates. In fact, doubling the aspect ratio cuts the induced drag in half. So, for slower and lower powered aircraft such as motorgliders and sailplanes, as well as powered hang gliders, a long span, high aspect ratio wing is necessary to minimize induced drag. The faster an aircraft cruises however, the less important induced drag becomes, making lower aspect ratios acceptable.

Wing planform also plays a part in determining the induced drag inherent in a wing. According to aerodynamic theory, the ideal wing will have an elliptical planform—the WWII Spitfire employed such a planform. From a manufacturing point of view an elliptical wing is expensive, so it's very seldom employed. Fortunately though, a linearly tapered wing can be nearly as efficient as an elliptical wing, about 99% or so, and a lot less expensive to produce. Theoretically, the best taper ratio for a wing seems to be for a tip chord/root chord ratio of .4. Even so, a simple rectangular wing can have 94% of an elliptical's efficiency and is very easy to manufacture, as well as being more stall resistant, as we shall discover later.

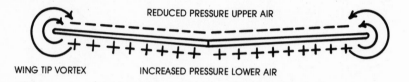

Fig. 7-10. The pressure field around a wing gives rise to tip vortices (the high pressure bottom air flows around the tips to the low pressure upper air) and induced drag.

Reduction of Induced Drag

There are various methods for reducing induced drag—all aimed at minimizing the wing tip vortices and the energy they absorb. Before we can reduce the impact of these vortices, however, we must have an understanding of their formation. As lift is generated the air below the wing is slightly above static pressure while the air above is slightly below static pressure. Since air flows from positive to negative pressure regions, it tends to "leak" around the wing tips in a circular pattern, forming the tip vortex. This leads to a slight spanwise flow of air as well—the air flows toward the tip on the bottom, and away from the tip on top.

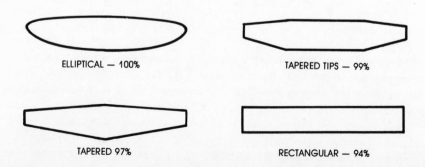

ig. 7-11. Basic wing planforms and their relative efficiency as lifting surfaces, at an aspect ratio of 7.

Results from wind tunnel tests offer some interesting conclusions. They have shown that the optimum wing shape has a moderately tapered planform, and a rounded negatively raked tip with the underside tapered to meet the top.

The latest development in the war against induced drag is the NASA developed winglet, which is incorporated in at least one ultralight, the Goldwing. Winglets are a refinement of the simple tip plate concept, which never really proved successful— seems as though any reduction in induced drag was cancelled out by increases in parasite drag.

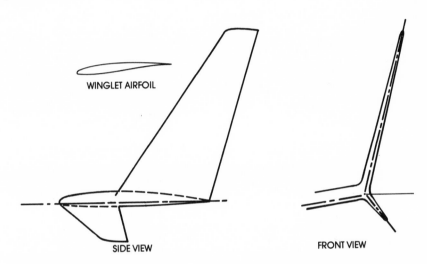

WINGLET AIRFOIL

SIDE VIEW

FRONT VIEW

Fig. 7-12. The NASA-developed winglet is the latest device for reducing induced drag.

In order for a winglet to function properly, it must be precisely designed and tested. The object is to alter the wing's lift distribution and the structure of the wing tip vortices. An analysis of the aerodynamics involved leads to the following conclusions: 1) C_D (coefficient of drag) decreases linearly with $C_L{}^2$—the slower you fly the more advantageous are winglets. 2) At low C_L's, i.e., high speeds, CD is increased where winglets are present. 3) High aspect ratio winglets are necessary. 4) Winglets should be placed aft of the wing tip high point to experience the strongest part of the tip vortex. 5) Winglets are most effective on wings with relatively high loadings. If a wing has a lot of washout or the planform is rectangular, the tip loading will not be relatively high. Therefore, winglets would be most effective on tapered wings, with minimal washout. In general, for winglets to be effective on an ultralight, a good deal of engineering is required. If nothing else, wing tip vertical surfaces can be very effective yaw stabilizers, as well as rudders.

Induced drag can be reduced quite easily simply by adding to the span and increasing the aspect ratio. The problem here is that the wing bending moment will also increase, requiring a stronger, heavier wing, making the gains questionable.

Induced Drag And Ground Effect

When an aircraft flies near the ground, within about one-half of its wingspan, the pilot will notice that he can fly on less power while his glide seems to improve. This is known as ground effect—the proximity of the ground causes a reduction in induced drag. The mechanism at work here is that the downwash angle is reduced

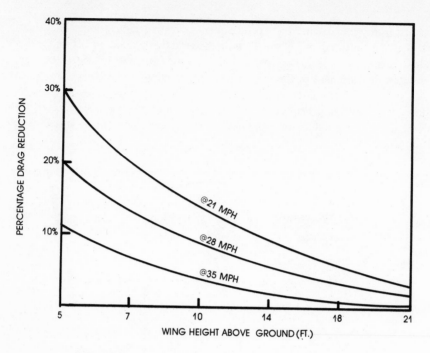

Fig. 7-13. How ground effect reduces induced drag.

or bounced back, tending to increase the effective aspect ratio. Some pilots like to say the air is "pressurized" between the wing and the ground, "cushioning" the landing!

Airplane Drag Analysis

Let's take a look at a typical wire braced ultralight to see the make up of its drag. First, we'll list the basic drag producing components.

1. landing gear
2. engine
3. fuselage tubing
4. bracing cables
5. tail surfaces
6. pilot cage
7. wing
8. pilot

Depending on the airspeed you're flying, of course, will determine the amount of drag. The faster you fly above and below minimum sink speed, the higher the drag. Not so obvious is the fact that as you change speed, you also change the drag percentages shared between parasite and induced. At the best glide ratio speed, the parasite and induced drags each make up half the total drag. At cruising speeds, on the other hand, the parasite drag climbs to around 90% of the total, leaving only 10% for induced. Again, high AR's (Aspect Ratio's) are for low speeds, while lower AR's are acceptable for cruising.

Now we can list the various components and their contributions to parasite and total drag.

Component	% Total Gliding Drag	% of Total Cruising Drag
Landing Gear	1.5	2.1
Engine	4.2	5.9
Bracing Cables	6.2	8.7
Tail Surfaces	.8	1.1
Pilot Cage	2.3	3.2
Pilot	10.0	14.0
Wing (profile)	25.0	55.0
Wing (induced)	50.0	10.0

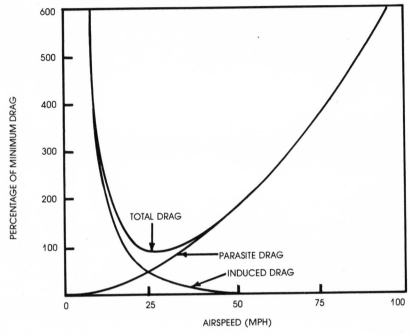

Fig. 7-14. How ultralight drags vary with airspeed.

Study of the drag table reveals the importance of streamlining as airspeeds increase. The wing profile drag and the parasite drag of the other components take on a greater significance. Conversely, the importance of aspect ratio decreases with speed, since induced drag is such a low percentage of the total. If our cable braced, tubing strewn powered glider were turned into a strut braced ultralight airplane, the total drag could be cut by perhaps 50%. If it were replaced by a cantilever design, the drag could be cut in half or more again. Streamlining then translates into an overall improvement in efficiency, which means greater speeds, flatter glides and lowered fuel consumption or less power required.

To keep drag at a minimum requires attention to the little details of ultralight design. Control surface gaps should be sealed, not only for reduced drag, but for increased control effectiveness as well. Engines should be cowled, at least somewhat. Protuberances should be avoided and intersecting surfaces minimized. If a manufacturer expects to remain competitive he'll have to "clean up his act." We shall all benefit by getting better performing aircraft as well as more beautiful designs.

Chapter Eight
The Ultralight Wing

The airfoil and its three dimensional counterpart, the wing, is one of man's most remarkable inventions—almost as significant as the wheel. It's development began occur until the experiments of Lilienthal and the Wright Brothers—that is when the value of curved surfaces was finally appreciated. Sure, inclined flat planes could lift, but only a fraction as much as those properly curved.

Since the experiments of the early aviation pioneers, thousands of different airfoils have been designed and tested, and a relatively few have seen application in aircraft. Sections have been designed for low drag, high lift, long range, high speed, high lift over drag ratios, low sink rates, high strength lightweight wings, etc. And now, with the advent of the ultralight, designers are looking to apply airfoils to the forgotten realm of low speed flight.

The pioneers developed wing sections solely by experimental means, often using birds' wings as models. Small scale wind tunnel testing was also done and naturally led to relatively thin cambered wings. Those early tests were done at very low Reynolds Numbers (100,000 or so) which, while great for the birds and small models, produced airfoils inferior for full scale aircraft.

As aircraft were developed for higher speeds, airfoils lost their undercamber. Airframes became aerodynamically cleaner as cable bracing diminished in favor of structural elements enclosed completely within the wing itself. This development eliminated the need for low RN data. But, when the modern ultralight appeared, the need for aerodynamic data in the RN range of 500,000 to 1,500,000 became acute.

The Airfoil

In general, an airfoil is any structure shaped to get a useful reaction from its passage through the air. More specifically, it is normally thought of as the cross-sectional shape of wings, tails, stabilizers, struts and even fuselages. It is designed to envelop the necessary structural elements while producing maximum lift and minimum drag.

To be effective, an ultralight airfoil needs a rounded leading edge, a relatively thin trailing edge and a fineness ratio of between 5 and 10. The thinness is dictated by structural requirements while attempting to minimize drag. The specific shape of a wing's airfoil is not all that critical in tailed designs, performance being more

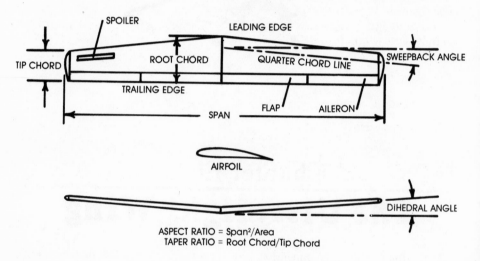

ASPECT RATIO = Span²/Area
TAPER RATIO = Root Chord/Tip Chord

Fig. 8-1. The defining geometry of a wing.

dependent on the wing's geometry. For canard and especially tailless designs however, the airfoil is quite critical because of the pitching moment, which is crucial to stability.

Before we get into airfoils per se, let's define a basic wing, its geometry and components. The illustration above shows the top view, or planform, front view and a cross-section or airfoil. The length from tip to tip is called the span, b. The width of the wing is its chord, which can vary from the center or root, c_r, to the tip, c_t. The wing area S, can be obtained by multiplying the average or mean chord $\bar{c}$, by the wingspan.

The taper ratio of a wing is the root chord divided by the tip chord. Aspect ratio is the span squared divided by the wing area. For a rectangular wing, the taper ratio is one, while the aspect ratio is simply the wingspan divided by the chord.

The sweepback angle, is traditionally defined as the angle the quarter chord line makes with a perpendicular to the root chord. Sweepback angle can also refer to the angle the leading edge makes with a perpendicular to the root chord.

110

The trailing edge of a wing is normally fitted with control surfaces comprising as much as 25% or so, of the wing's area. The outer half of the wing contains the ailerons which are used for roll control during a bank and turn. They deflect differentially only—the up aileron to the inside of the turn and the down aileron to the outside of the turn.

The inner half of the wing carries flaps which are used to alter the coefficients of lift and drag by a simultaneous down deflection. They are normally used on approach to landing to lower the landing speed, while increasing the glide angle. They can also be used for takeoff, at smaller angular deflections, to shorten the takeoff run. Flaps cannot be deflected differentially.

In some instances, ailerons and flaps are combined into a single surface per wing half, called a flaperon. They can be moved differentially as well as in unison to serve the function of both ailerons and flaps. However, they compromise the ultimate effectiveness of individual surfaces. Flaperons can also be deflected up slightly, with the potential of decreasing drag at cruise.

Some ultralight wings also include spoilers—board-like surfaces located aft the airfoil's high point—for roll control. They normally lie flush with the upper wing surface, but when actuated, they open broadside to the airflow causing early separation, a loss of lift and an increase in drag.

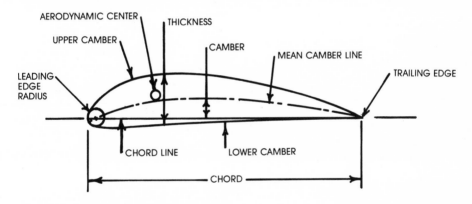

Fig. 8-2. Defining sketch of a typical airfoil section.

Other ultralight wings may incorporate tip draggers, winglets, stabilator type control surfaces or any combination of these. But, all are appendages and not part of the wing itself. We shall cover them in detail in the stability and control section.

Now let's take a look at some airfoil basics, assuming an infinitely long, constant chord wing. This enables us to ignore the certain effects of a real, three dimensional wing, while allowing an understanding of the fundamentals of wing aerodynamics.

Airfoil Geometry

At this point, it is useful to define a basic airfoil in terms of its geometry. The illustration shows a typical low speed airfoil section. The length from leading edge, LE, to trailing edge, TE, is the chord, c. The greatest distance between the upper and lower surfaces is the thickness, which is typically stated as a percentage of the chord, or the ratio t/c. (It's the reciprocal of fineness ratio.) The mean line is

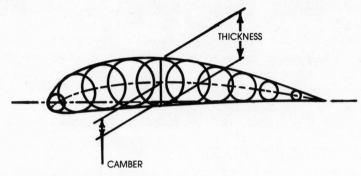

Fig. 8-3. A definition of thickness and camber.

simply the line halfway between the upper and lower cambers. The leading edge radius describes the leading edge circle whose center is on the mean line. The mean line could also be defined as the locus of centers of circles drawn inside the section. In this case the thickness would be represented by the largest diameter circle. The aerodynamic center is that chordwise position (approx. at quarter chord) where the total lift and drag can be assumed to occur, as well as the point about which the pitching moment coefficient is constant.

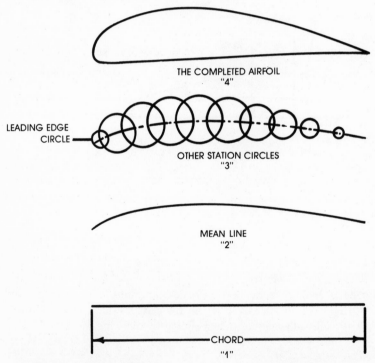

THE COMPLETED AIRFOIL
"4"

LEADING EDGE
CIRCLE

OTHER STATION CIRCLES
"3"

MEAN LINE
"2"

CHORD
"1"

Fig. 8-4. Constructing an airfoil section.

AIRFOIL FAMILIES

Geometrically, an airfoil can be defined as a mean line with a superimposed thickness distribution. Aerodynamically, the mean line determines the basic characteristics, which are modified slightly by the thickness. This fact leads us to believe that airfoil geometries can be systematized into "families" of sections, which is exactly what the NACA (National Advisory Committee for Aeronautics—now NASA) did during the 30's and 40's.

The Four-Digit Series

In 1933, the NACA published its so-called four-digit series of airfoils. These were not based on any theoretical considerations, but rather evolved out of the

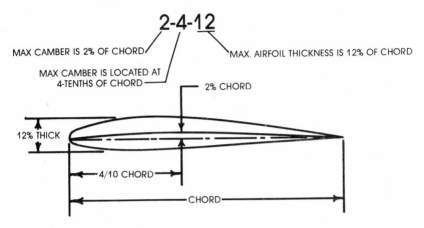

Fig. 8-5. The NACA 2412 is a good example of a four-digit series airfoil.

good wing sections of the time. The NACA found that by varying an airfoil's thickness and camber, and their distribution along the chord, they could generate an entire family of sections.

The four-digit series was based on the maximum airfoil thickness being located at 30% chord. This location was believed superior, based on the empirical results of the day. Thickness ratios ran from 6% to 21%. Camber ratios ranged from 0% to 7%, with high points located between 20% and 70% of chord.

The four numbers used in the four digit series defined an airfoil like this: the first digit gave the percentage of camber, the second the location of the maximum camber in tenths of the chord, while the last two numbers represent the maximum thickness in percent of chord. An example of this series is the 2412 airfoil.

The Five-Digit Series

In an effort to increase the maximum lift coefficient while reducing the pitching moment, the five-digit series was developed. The mean line was curved up to the 20% chord point, then made straight to the trailing edge. The thickness distribution was the same as for the four-digit series. The numbering system of the five-digit series is a little more involved than the four-digit series. The first digit is the maximum height of the mean line in percent chord, which multiplied by 15 gives the "design" lift coefficient. The second digit is twice the maximum camber location in tenths chord. The third digit refers to the shape of the after portion of the mean line—zero means it is straight. The last two digits represent the maximum thickness in percent chord. An example of the five-digit series is the 23012 section.

Other Airfoil Families

The NACA developed other airfoil series, but these were for higher speed applications and of little use to ultralights. The sixteen series were the first to be

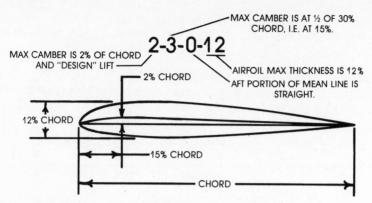

Fig. 8-6. The NACA 23012 is an example of the five-digit series airfoils.

designed around theoretical considerations with the minimum pressure point at 60% chord. The camber lines were configured for a uniform pressure difference. The series has been widely used in both marine and aircraft propellers.

The six-series airfoils, the so-called laminar flow sections, were designed to achieve low drag with good lift. These airfoils we characterized by a maximum thickness located further aft than for the four and five digit series, resulting in extensive laminar flow and low skin friction drag. The trouble with these sections is

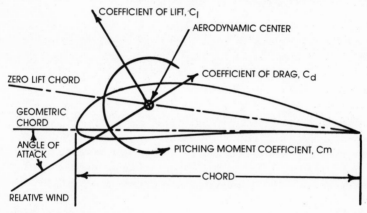

Fig. 8-7. The forces acting on an airfoil.

that unless they are built and maintained in an absolutely pristine smooth condition, the laminar flow turns turbulent, making them no better than the older airfoils. For instance, crushed insects on the leading edge are enough to destroy laminar flow.

Airfoil Characteristics

The three main characteristics of an airfoil are lift, drag, and pitching moment. They depend on the shape and thickness of the airfoil and are plotted on a graph, versus angle of attack. These characteristics also depend on the Reynolds Number which is more important to ultralights than to heavier, faster aircraft. Aspect ratio and planform are important in determining the characteristics of a three dimensional wing.

As an airfoil moves relative to the air, pressure differences arise between the

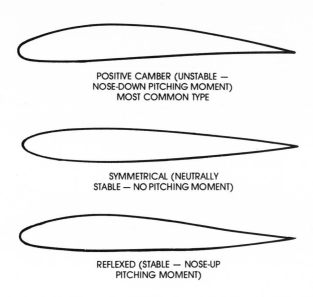

POSITIVE CAMBER (UNSTABLE —
NOSE-DOWN PITCHING MOMENT)
MOST COMMON TYPE

SYMMETRICAL (NEUTRALLY
STABLE — NO PITCHING MOMENT)

REFLEXED (STABLE — NOSE-UP
PITCHING MOMENT)

Fig. 8-8. The basic types of airfoils.

upper and lower surfaces, resulting in lift, drag, and a negative pitching moment. If the relative wind strikes it parallel to the zero lift chord however, it will develop no lift, at some negative angle of attack. Yes, a positively cambered airfoil begins to lift at some negative angle. It all depends on the shape of the mean line. A symmetrical airfoil, which has a straight mean line (no curvature) and equal upper and lower cambers develops no lift at zero angle of attack. It generates lift at negative angles just as well as at positive angles, and has a zero pitching moment.

An airfoil with a reflexed mean line will develop a positive pitching moment, i.e., it will tend to nose up. Reflexed sections are stable and have been used on

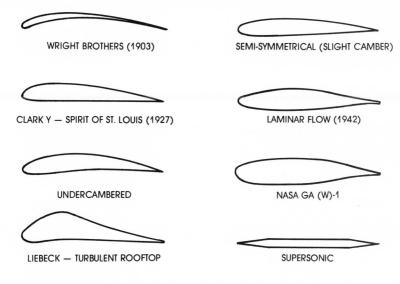

WRIGHT BROTHERS (1903)

SEMI-SYMMETRICAL (SLIGHT CAMBER)

CLARK Y — SPIRIT OF ST. LOUIS (1927)

LAMINAR FLOW (1942)

UNDERCAMBERED

NASA GA (W)-1

LIEBECK — TURBULENT ROOFTOP

SUPERSONIC

Fig. 8-9. Other types of airfoils.

flying wings with no sweepback. The turned-up trailing edge, in effect, replaces the horizontal tail, but it creates drag in doing so—you cannot get stability without paying for it, as with everything else in aircraft design.

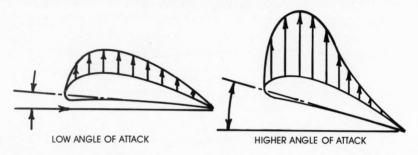

LOW ANGLE OF ATTACK   HIGHER ANGLE OF ATTACK

Fig. 8-10. Pressure distribution changes with angle of attack.

The Meaning of Airfoil Characteristic Curves

The lift curve, C_1, begins as soon as the airfoil is tilted up from the zero lift angle. After this, it continues to rise in practically a straight line until it reaches about 10½ degrees. Here, the lift levels off and then starts to fall with increasing angle of attack—that's a stall. The slope of the lift curve generally runs around a C_1 of .1 per degree of angle of attack. Lower the Reynolds Number and the maximum possible lift drops, the drop off in C_1 becomes less pronounced (meaning a gentler stall), while the slope remains the same.

The rounding of the top of the lift curve with decreasing Reynolds Number is exactly why most ultralights go into a high sink rate mush, rather than falling out of the air, as do higher RN aircraft. The higher sink rate is the result of drag

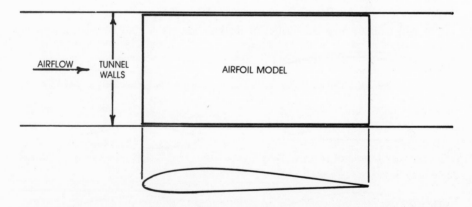

AIRFLOW   TUNNEL WALLS   AIRFOIL MODEL

Fig. 8-11. How two-dimensional flow is simulated in a wind tunnel to obtain airfoil section characteristics.

increasing with angle of attack, as the curve depicts. The lowered RN of ultralight flight means higher coefficients of drag.

The lowered RN also has little or no effect on the pitching moment characteristics of most airfoils that might be employed on an ultralight.

A plot of C_1 over C_d results in the lift to drag ratio of the airfoil. At some low angle of attack, say 2 or 3 degrees, this ratio is a maximum and that is where

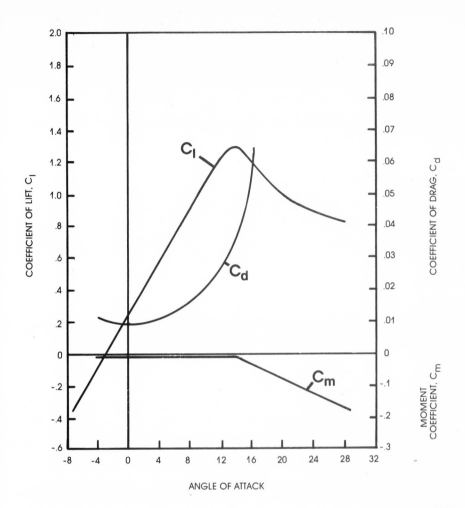

Fig. 8-12. Aerodynamic characteristics for NACA 23012 airfoil section at a Reynolds Number of 665,000 (near the stall speed of an ultralight).

an aircraft ought to be designed to cruise—the most lift for the least drag. In general, the C_l/C_d decreases with decreasing Reynolds Numbers, and the cruising C_l is caused to increase—meaning that higher angles of attack are required for best efficiency at lower speeds. In other words, the "optimum" C_l increases with decreasing Reynolds Number.

Very Low Reynolds Numbers Airfoils

The Reynolds Numbers are very low for insects, model airplanes, birds and small diameter (3 foot) propeller blades. Typical values were listed earlier in the text. But, to give you some idea of how thin sections perform, a figure is presented. It shows that flat plates and circular arcs outperform airfoils at the lower Reynolds Numbers, but the airfoil becomes superior as the RN increases.

Effects of Airfoil Geometry on Characteristics

Besides Reynolds Number, the characteristics of an airfoil are affected by thickness and camber and their distribution along the chord. Airfoil characteristics

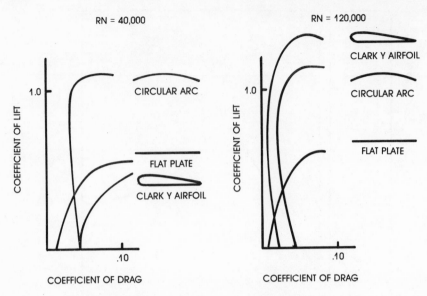

RN = 40,000

RN = 120,000

Fig. 8-13. Lift and drag characteristics of thin sections at very low Reynolds Numbers.

can also be altered by the addition of flaps and slats, primarily to increase the coefficient of lift.

Perhaps the single most important characteristic of an airfoil is the shape of its lift curve. If it drops off sharply after its maximum, the aircraft will have a very pronounced stall break. The nose will want to fall through abruptly. If the leading edge is sharp, you can bet the aircraft will have a sharp stall. The cure for this undesirable trait is to increase the leading edge nose radius to round the lift curve and produce a gentle stall of mush type characteristic.

Sections with high cambers produce higher lift and a broader angle of attack range.

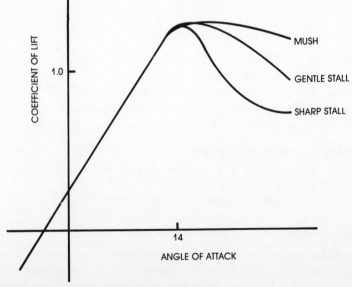

Fig. 8-14. The three basic types of airfoil stall.

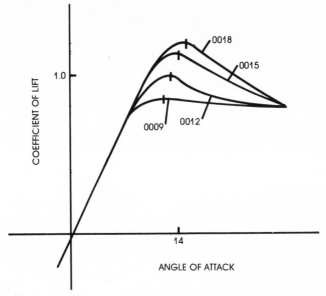

Fig. 8-15. How thickness affects symmetrical airfoil lift characteristics at an ultralight stall Reynolds Number of 700,000. Thick airfoil produce more lift at a higher angle of attack. The thinnest airfoil has the gentlest stall.

Along with that comes a gentler stall, but an increased nose down pitching moment. Thick, higher cambered airfoils are generally used on sailplanes. Thin higher cambered airfoil are commonly used on model sailplanes, for thinner sections are

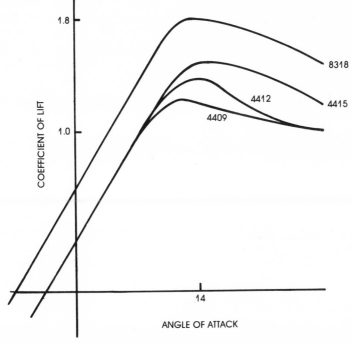

Fig. 8-16. How camber and thickness variations affect the lift characteristics of an ultralight stall Reynolds Number of 700,000. Thicker airfoils generate more lift and a broader useful angle of attack range. The more forward camber of the 8318 lowered the angle for maximum lift as well as the zero lift angle.

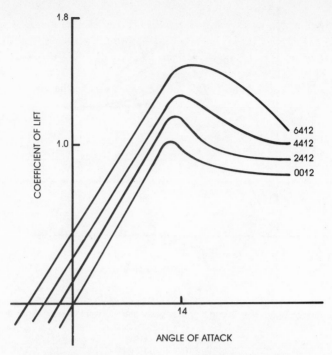

Fig. 8-17. How camber affects lift characteristics at an ultralight stall Reynolds Number of 700,000. Higher cambers produce higher lift, a broader angle of attack range and, a gentler stall.

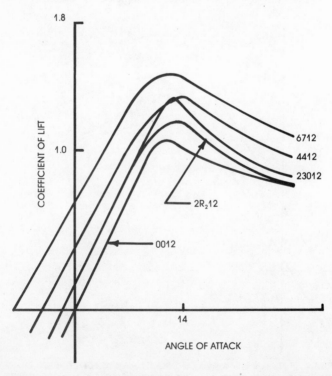

Fig. 8-18. How variations in mean line shape affect lift characteristics at an ultralight stall Reynolds Number of 700,000.

more efficient at very low Reynolds Numbers. Higher camber is evident on many single surface airfoil ultralights, resulting in slower cruising speeds. Stalls are quite gentle because of the lower Reynolds Numbers. Higher cambered airfoil tend to be "one speeded" in that they are efficient in only a very narrow angle of attack range. Also, the further forward the maximum camber, the less the pitching moment.

Regarding thickness, the optimum thickness for a 4- or 5-digit ultralight airfoil appears to be around 14% or so at a Reynolds Number of 1,000,000. As Reynolds numbers increase to 8,000,000, the optimum thickness decreases to around 11%. Fortunately, structural requirements favor the thicker sections, especially when the designer is going for a cantilever wing; the thickness allows for a deeper, stronger, and lighter spar.

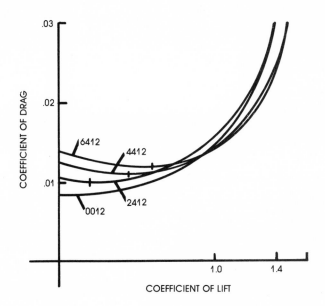

Fig. 8-19. Camber raises airfoil profile drag at an ultralight cruise Reynolds Number of 2,300,000. The minimum drag moves to higher lift coefficients as camber increases.

High Lift

One way to achieve higher lift is to increase camber and thickness, while moving the maximum camber point aft somewhat. NACA did this with their 6712 and 8318 airfoils. As might be expected, the sharped nosed 6712 has the sharper stall, while the 8318's is gentle. As would be expected, these sections do offer increased drag as well as higher pitching moments. A more recently developed airfoil, the FX-MS-150A develops very high lift at ultralight Reynolds numbers, while maintaining relatively low drag. The price for this, however, is a large pitching moment and a very sharp stall.

The newest, most radical high lift, low Reynolds Number airfoil ever designed is the Liebeck type, patented by McDonnel–Douglas Corporation. At first glance it appears to be contrary to most good airfoil design thinking. It has a 10% cambered mean line with the aft portion reflexed, a 20% thickness, undercambered lower surface, and a large leading edge radius. As might not be expected, the drag is quite low, lower than the four-digit airfoils at the same Reynolds number; it has a sharp stall, but a very low pitching moment.

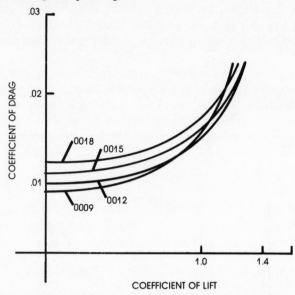

Fig. 8-20. Thickness raises airfoil profile drag with lift coefficient at an ultralight cruise Reynolds Number of 2,300,000.

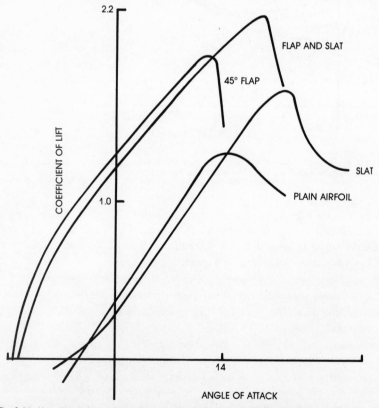

Fig. 8-21. How the slat and flap affect the lift coefficient of the Clark-Y airfoil.

To understand this airfoil, we must look at the boundary layer. It so happens that the reflexed upper surface actually does a better job in decelerating the airflow as it comes off the hump. Apparently, the airflow has enough extra momentum after rounding the hump so that it remains attached. The reflex, of course, also cuts the pitching moment down to size. And, while the stall break is very definite, recovery is also very sudden—a half degree nose down will reinstate the lift.

The Liebeck may have application to ultralights. It was designed for the proper Reynolds Numbers, and its thickness would allow strong, lightweight cantilever wings. It is covered by patents, however.

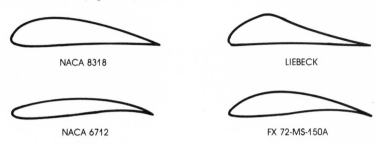

NACA 8318   LIEBECK

NACA 6712   FX 72-MS-150A

Fig. 8-22. Some high lift airfoils.

Other methods of increasing lift include slats and flaps. These allow using a "conventional" airfoil with a low pitching moment and gentle stall, while gaining the benefits of higher lift and drag when needed, as during approach to landing. Leading edge slats (jetliners use them) pop out of the upper surface leading edge to deflect high energy air on to the after upper surface allowing attached flow at higher angles of attack, resulting in more lift. Flaps are simply hinged trailing edges which increase lift and drag when deflected, as during approach to landing. Minimal flap settings of 10 to 15 degrees add more lift than drag, and can be used to shorten the takeoff run.

The Practical, 3-Dimensional Wing

As soon as an airfoil section is incorporated into a wing its efficiency decreases.

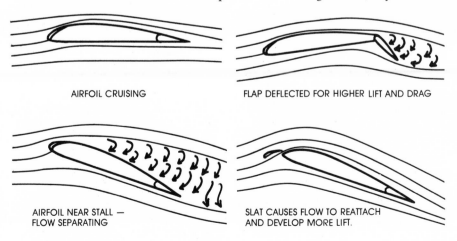

AIRFOIL CRUISING   FLAP DEFLECTED FOR HIGHER LIFT AND DRAG

AIRFOIL NEAR STALL —
FLOW SEPARATING   SLAT CAUSES FLOW TO REATTACH
AND DEVELOP MORE LIFT.

Fig. 8-23. Flaps and slats are used to increase lift.

Whereas two-dimensional airfoils can develop a C_1 of about 0.1 per degree angle of attack, wings are only capable of something less. While the maximum lift of the wing is as nearly as great as its airfoil's a greater angle of attack is needed to reach that lift. Let's find out why.

Airflow Around a Wing

As a wing moves through the air, secondary airflows are established along its surfaces. In addition to the lowered pressure on the upper surface and increased pressure on the lower surface, slight spanwise flows are set up. Unlike our two-dimensional wing of infinite aspect ratio, a real wing has tips—tips for the lower surface's high pressure air to flow around and up into the low pressure air on the upper surface. This means the air on the bottom of the wing actually flows toward the tip, while the air on top of the wing flows toward the center of the wing. These two opposing spanwise airflows meet at the trailing edge and form vortices that eventually bundle together into one large vortex with a core span somewhat less than the geometric span. In other words, a wing can be thought of as a lifting line with

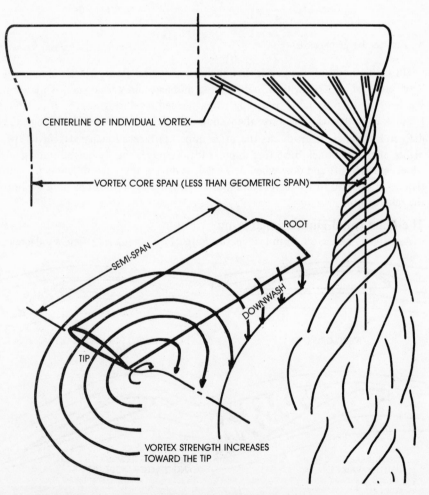

Fig. 8-24. A lifting wing experiences spanwise flows and develops tip vortices.

the geometric span. In other words, a wing can be thought of as a lifting line with two "bound" vortices trailing behind.

Naturally, as the tip is approached, the pressure differences between the upper and lower surfaces are trying to equalize—at the tip the lift is zero. This might lead

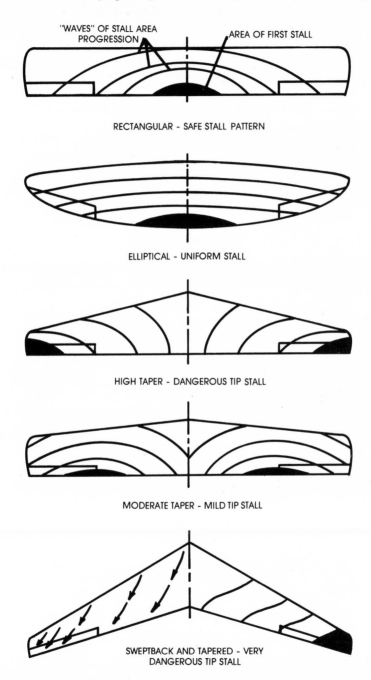

Fig. 8-25. Initial stall patterns for various wing planforms with no twist. Adding twist (wash out) will drive the stall inboard.

us to believe that we could remove some of the tip! Indeed, we could, and improve the wing's efficiency i.e., reduce its induced drag.

Wing theory tells us that the most efficient wing planform is elliptical. It allows an ideal drop in the pressure difference as the tip is approached, resulting in an elliptical lift distribution and minimal tip vortices. Elliptical wings however, are difficult and expensive to manufacture, so we rarely see any. (The WW II Spitfire had one.)

An alternative to the elliptical wing is the tapered wing which is almost as efficient, and a lot easier to produce. Furthermore, the reduced tip chords reduce the loading toward the tip, lowering the structural requirements inboard, particularly for cantilevered wings. The coefficient of lift is now more uniform over the whole span because the tip vortices are weaker.

If the taper ratio is high to where the chord decreases faster than the lift (i.e., the downwash angle is not reduced toward the tip), the coefficient of lift near the tip may actually increase. This forces the tip to carry a disproportionately greater share of the total lift causing it to stall first. This is a dangerous situation, because if a tip stalls first, the aircraft can enter a spin quite easily. Furthermore, since the ailerons are located near the tip, they become useless when the tip stalls, eliminating lateral control.

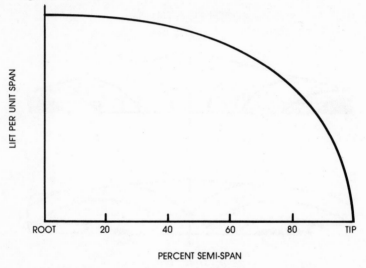

Fig. 8-26. Typical span loading distribution.

A reasonable compromise is a slightly tapered wing since it provides a better lift distribution with the wing stalling inboard of the tips first, while creating less induced drag. If the wing is twisted with washout at the tips, the stall pattern can be modified to approach that of a rectangular wing. The optimum taper ratio is for a tip chord of forty percent of the root chord.

A sweptback wing has the worst stall pattern of all. The sweepback causes a spanwise flow toward the tip, leading to a tip that stalls first. Flow fences, as mentioned previously, and washed-out tips are the only cure for this problem.

As it turns out, the aerodynamically inferior, lowly looking rectangular wing has a lot going for it in the stall department. Mind you, it is not as efficient as the

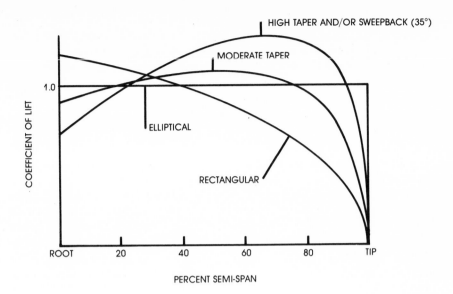

Fig. 8-27. Spanwise distribution of lift coefficient.

tapered wing, but it has a friendly stall pattern—the root stalls first, the tips last. A stall beginning at the root allows the aircraft to drop straight through, with no tendency to drop a wing.

Another way to fight tip stall, with any planform, is to twist the wing. In other words, build it with the tips at less of an angle than the root airfoil. This way the tip will fly while the root stalls first. This technique, called washout, costs something in profile drag (induced drag is reduced, though), but it is necessary to produce good stall characteristics. Most aircraft use washout.

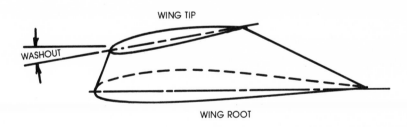

Fig. 8-28. End view of tapered wing with washout. Sight down most any wing and you'll likely see it is "washed out".

The Influence of Bodies Near The Wing

The lift distribution of a wing alone is nearly elliptical, but as soon as a body is placed near the wing, that changes. Furthermore, placing a body on top of a wing is more damaging than placing it below. It stands to reason, since the upper surface of a wing generates a larger percentage of lift than the bottom. Plain and simple, high winged aircraft tend to be more efficient than low wingers. If we examine the lift distribution in these cases, we can see why; the continuity is destroyed with a

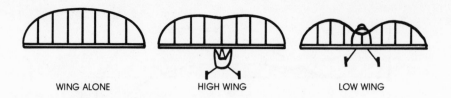

Fig. 8-29. The presence of a body near a wing disturbs the lift distribution and lowers its efficiency.

body on top of the wing. In effect, a loss of wing area is created. The placement of engines is also important here. Under wing arrangements are superior.

The Influence of Aspect Ratio

An airfoil is a wing with an infinite aspect ratio—it has no tip, no tip vortices and no induced drag. A real wing, of course, has a finite aspect ratio and all the vortices and drag that go along with it. A smaller aspect ratio allows the tip and its vortices to have a greater effect on the wing's operation—they become proportionately larger. The secondary spanwise flows become more important. The effective angle of attack is reduced. But the "bottom line" shows up in the airfoil's characteristics.

Lowering the aspect ratio from infinity down through three has some negative effects on the two-dimensional airfoil characteristics: 1) the slope of the lift curve

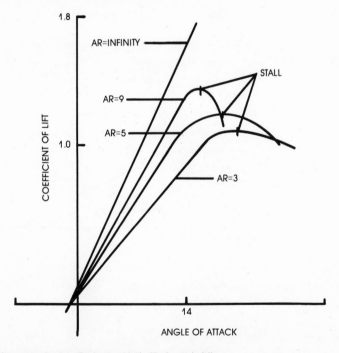

Fig. 8-30. How aspect ratio affects an airfoil's lift characteristics.

decreases. This means that instead of getting a C_1 of .1 for each degree of angle of attack, we get somewhat less, but the stall angle increases. 2) The maximum lift attainable is less, but lower aspects have a gentler stall. 3) With finite aspect ratios comes the addition of induced drag; the smaller the aspect, the higher the drag. The only airfoil characteristic that aspect ratio doesn't affect is the pitching moment—it remains constant.

The net effect of a wing's three-dimensional airflows, its location on a fuselage and any engines it may carry, can be expressed by a factor, "e," known as the Oswald efficiency factor. Multiplying a wing's geometric aspect by e yields the "effective"

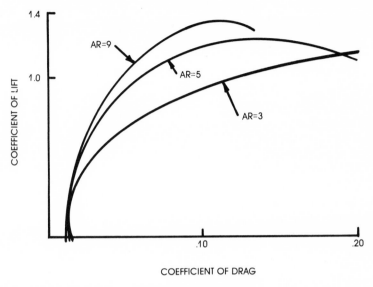

Fig. 8-31. How aspect ratio affects an airfoil's drag characteristics.

aspect ratio. Even though a wing may have a geometric aspect of say 20, its effective aspect may only be 8, or even less! In other words, e tells us how efficient a wing is. For example, most high wing general aviation type aircraft have e's of around 0.8, while low wings yield about 0.6. Since ultralights have relatively small "fuselages," compared to the wing, larger values of e could be expected on a clean design.

Mean Aerodynamic Chord

The airfoil section in a wing where all the wing's aerodynamic forces and moments can be assumed to act is called the Mean Aerodynamic Chord or M.A.C.

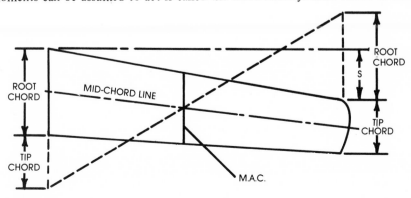

Fig. 8-32. Geometric determination of the Mean Aerodynamic Chord.

129

Its aerodynamic center is critical to all performance and stability and control problems. It can be located as shown in the figure.

A Summary of Airfoil and Wing Characteristics

- The maximum lift coefficient decreases with decreasing Reynolds number.
- The minimum drag coefficient decreases with Reynolds number.
- The stall becomes more gentle with decreasing Reynolds number.
- Pitching moments remain relatively constant with Reynolds Number. That is, the tendency for a wing to nose-up or down is unaffected by RN changes.
- The optimum lift coefficient increases with decreasing Reynolds number and increasing camber.
- Increased thickness increases the maximum lift coefficient as well as the stall angle.
- Increased camber produces a higher maximum lift coefficient a higher stall angle, and a gentler stall.
- The section lift curve slope remains relatively constant for moderately thick (15%) airfoils in the ultralight Reynolds number range.
- Airfoil section minimum profile drag coefficients increase with thickness and camber.
- Section lift curve slopes decrease with decreasing aspect ratio.
- Induced drag increases with decreasing aspect ratio.
- Lower aspect ratios tend to have a slightly lower maximum coefficient of lift while the stall angle of attack increases.
- Aspect ratio becomes less important with speed since induced drag decreases with speed.
- A rectangular wing stalls at the root first eliminating tip stall.
- A moderately tapered wing is the most efficient (next to an elliptical) and can avoid tip stall problems if washed-out.
- Double surfaced airfoils are superior to single surfaced airfoils in the ultralight Reynolds Number range.
- Squared-off wing tip planforms are as efficient as any.
- High wings are more efficient than low wings.
- Flaps can be used to increase the maximum lift and drag coefficients for landing and takeoff.
- The greater the sweepback the lower the maximum lift coefficient and the less steep the lift curve slope. Non-swept wings give the best lift.

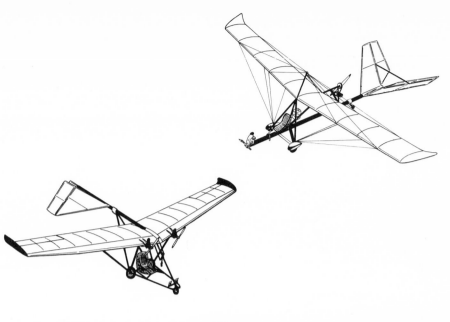

Section Three
ULTRALIGHT HANDLING QUALITIES

Introduction

Ultralight Handling Qualities

Introduction

A primary goal for any ultralight aircraft engineer is to design an airplane that is pleasant to fly. All recreational pilots want an airplane that is inherently stable and easy to control—an airplane with nice handling qualities.

Ultralight stability depends on a number of variable and interrelated factors. It is possible to design an airplane that flys straight and level without the pilot having to control it. It is also possible to make it so stable that the pilot has a tough time maneuvering it. That, we don't want. What we do want, is an airplane that can return to straight and level flight automatically, after having been upset by a gust or other disturbance. In other words, a pilot wants an airplane that flys itself when he lets go of the controls, yet responds well to his control inputs.

Another way of stating the problem of designing an airplane with nice handling qualities is to say that it is a battle between stability and maneuverability. If an aircraft is too stable, it will be less maneuverable. If it is not stable enough, it will require constant attention in the control department. Both situations are undesirable, meaning that a compromise is necessary to design an airplane that is stable yet maneuverable. When the compromise is optimized, you will have an airplane with nice handling qualities.

To gain an appreciation of what goes into making an aircraft pleasant to fly, let's take a closer look at the subject of stability and control.

Reference Axes

Unlike surface conveyances, which are limited to two-dimensional movement, aircraft are free to move about in all three dimensions. In addition to moving straight ahead, side to side, and up and down, an ultralight is capable of making

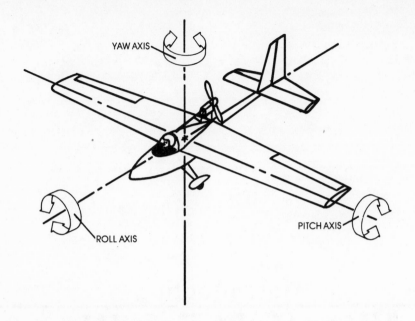

Fig. A-3. The reference axes of an ultralight.

three fundamental motions, one about each of its three axes. The three axes/motions are pitch, roll and yaw.

The pitch, or lateral, axis is an imaginery line that runs through the center of gravity, parallel to the wing. Rotation about this axis produces changes in pitch attitude, i.e., nose up and nose down. Pitch angle is controlled by the elevator, taking on a fixed attitude depending on elevator setting.

The roll, or longitudinal, axis is an imaginary line that runs from the nose of the aircraft through its CG and is parallel to the direction of flight. Motions around this axis are governed primarily by the ailerons which, when deflected, set up a rate of roll rather than a fixed degree—ailerons are rate controls. Once the desired bank

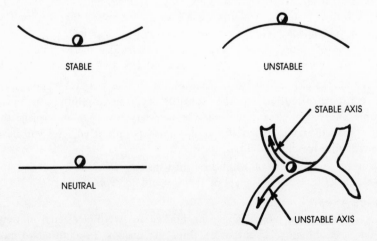

Fig. B-3. The three degrees of stability.

134

angle is achieved by aileron deflection, the ailerons are neutralized or even reversed, to maintain the desired angle. Constant aileron deflection would cause the bank angle to increase, and continue at a particular rate.

The yaw, or vertical axis is an imaginary line passing through the CG perpendicular to the other two axes. Rudder controls yaw, a given rudder deflection resulting in a particular yaw rate.

STABILITY

In order for an ultralight to be pleasant to fly, it must possess certain handling qualities. It should be capable of being flown hands-off for a short period of time, which implies that it is stable. But there is more to stability than that. In reality, there are three degrees of stability and two general types.

Positive Stability

Positive stability can be defined broadly as the ability of an aircraft to return to its original flight condition after having been disturbed from that condition.

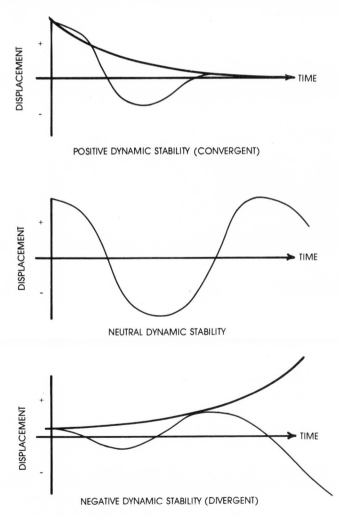

Fig. C-3. The three degrees of dynamic stability.

Equilibrium exists when all the forces acting on an aircraft, or any body, are balanced by equal and opposite forces. In order for an ultralight to be in equilibrium, lift must equal weight and thrust must equal drag. If these forces are not balanced, the aircraft will either accelerate or turn. A marble in a bowl would be a good example of positive stability—it wants to stay in the center.

Neutral Stability

Neutral stability is displayed when a body in equilibrium is disturbed and has no tendency to either return to its original position or condition, nor move further from it. It has no preference—it is neutrally stable. A marble on a flat horizontal surface would be neutrally stable.

Negative Stability

A body exhibits negative stability when, after having been disturbed from equilibrium, it has a tendency to move farther away from its original condition or position. Negative stability has no place in an ultralight! A marble resting on top of a bowling ball would be negatively stable.

Two Kinds of Stability

There are two kinds of stability: static stability and dynamic stability.

Static stability exists when an ultralight returns to its original position or condition, after the passage of a disturbance. Static instability would be where, after having encountered a disturbance, the ultralight would continue deviating from its original position or condition. Most ultralights today appear to be statically stable about all axes, some more than others.

Dynamic stability is a little more complicated situation since it involves oscillation, or a back and forth motion, that gradually lessens or dampens out with time, until the aircraft has returned to its original position or conditon. A pendulum would be dynamically stable, since the amplitude of its swing lessens with time. If the pendulum were immersed in water, the period of time for it to stop oscillating would be lessened. In other words, the water damps the motion.

Chapter Nine

Longitudinal Stability and Control

The traditional way of expressing static longitudinal stability is through the characteristics of pitching moment versus angle of attack. If the mean aerodynamic chord (M.A.C.) has an increasing nose down pitching moment with increasing angle of attack, it is considered stable. This is the basic criterion for a longitudinally stable airplane.

If an M.A.C. has a constant nose down pitching moment with increasing angle of attack, it is neutrally stable—it has a tendency to stay where it is put. Trouble is, it doesn't want to return to its original position. If a gust puts it into a dive, it stays in that dive until pulled out by the pilot. It has no desire to seek its original trim angle of attack and speed. A neutrally stable airplane must be flown (controlled) constantly—a very fatiguing task. A wing-only airplane with its center of gravity at its aerodynamic center would be neutrally stable. A modern fighter plane is neutrally stable, or maybe even negatively stable, to maximize its maneuverability. But, the pilot is aided by a computer that helps him fly the plane!

Negative stability occurs when the pitching moment becomes more positive with increasing angle of attack. In other words, the higher the nose goes, the higher it wants to go. Any object such as an engine nacelle or fuselage pod, forward

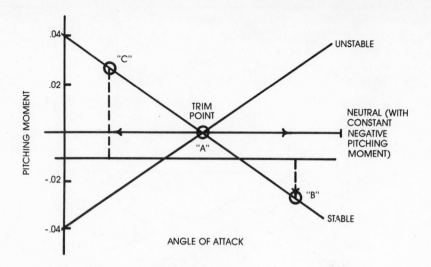

Fig. 9-1. Stability is determined by how an aircraft tends to pitch with changes in angle of attack.

of a wing's aerodynamic center is destabilizing in this manner. This should be readily apparent—an airplane with a long nose, flying in a nose high attitude would have the relative wind tending to push its nose up further still. To get rid of the neutral stability of our wing and the destabilizing affect of the engine nacelle the simplest thing we can do is to add a horizontal tail.

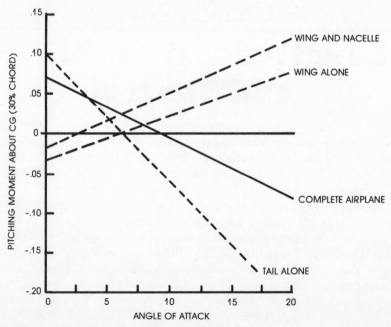

Fig. 9-2. Breakdown of typical ultralight longitudinal stability.

Now, suppose we are in straight and level flight at cruising speed and we're hit by a gust from below. This event momentarily increases the angle of attack from the original trim condition, point "A," to the point "B" condition. Here, a

138

negative pitching moment exists—the airplane wants to nose down to restore itself to its original trim point, "A." If the aircraft is hit with a gust from above, the angle of attack is reduced. The aircraft develops a positive pitching moment and noses up to point "C," in an effort to restore the original trim point, "A."

So how does a tail make an aircraft stable, you ask? The accompanying figure provides the answer. First of all, for an airplane to be in a stable, trimmed,

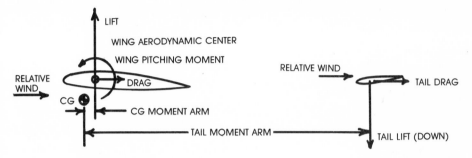

Fig. 9-3. The basic criteria for logitudinal stability in cruise.

equilibrium flight condition, it must be balanced at the CG (much like a see-saw) with the wing providing enough lift to equal the gross weight. This balance is achieved basically, when the sum of the wing pitching moment and CG moment arm times the gross weight is equal to the tail lift times the tail moment arm. For cruise, it is most desirable that equilibrium be established with minimal tail lift (which also means minimal trim drag.) In other words, a wing with minimal or zero pitching moment (or maybe even a positive pitching moment) is desirable, along with an airplane design that minimizes tail lift requirements.

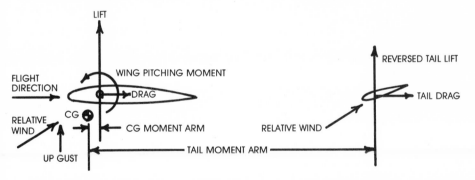

Fig. 9-4. A nose down pitching moment develops when an up gust hits a stable aircraft.

When the angle of attack is changed from the cruise trim condition, a new set of forces and moments is established. Let's take the case of a gust from below. Here, the wing lift is momentarily increased while the tail lift is momentarily reversed. The net effect is an increased nose down pitching moment and the aircraft's return to the original trim condition. (Notice why the tail's lift is reversed—The relative wind is giving it a positive angle of attack and up lift.)

Effect of Thrust Line and Propeller Location

As soon as you add power to the basic stability picture, things change, depending

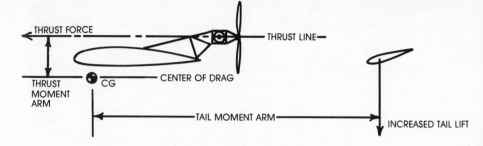

Fig. 9-5. A high thrust line develops a nose-down pitching moment that must be balanced by tail lift, adding to the trim drag. It's a stabilizing influence, however.

on the location of the thrust line. If the thrust line is through the center of drag and center of gravity, there will be no extra pitching moments generated—the designer's goal. If the thrust line is located somewhere else, then power changes will affect the equilibrium.

If our ultralight has its propeller located way above the CG and center of drag, then trim changes will occur with different power settings. When power is increased, the thrust will tend to nose down the aircraft, and vice versa. This is undesirable and should not exist in any ultralight you may fly. An unawareness of the importance of thrust line location caused problems during the mid 1970's on some early powered hang gliders. Rogallos with king post and keel mounted propellers, as well as Easy Risers with improper thrust line inclinations caused "unexplained" diving problems under power.

A high thrust line is a stabilizing influence, in that it develops a nose down pitching moment. Take the case of slow flight. Here, the forward speed is low,

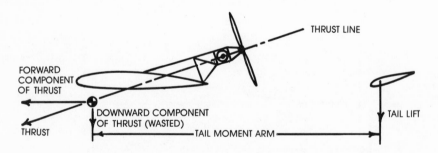

Fig. 9-6. Tilting the thrust line so it passes through the CG and center of drag will eliminate trim changes with power setting changes, but some thrust is wasted.

therefore the thrust is high (thrust is generally maximum under static conditions.) the basic criterion for stability is met—as the angle of attack increases (i.e., as we slow down) the nose-down pitching moment increases. This is fine, but a larger tail is required to develop the increased tail lift needed to maintain equilibrium under slow-speed, high-thrust conditions.

Propeller location also affects stability. A tractor configuration is destabilizing to the extent that 2% of the aircraft's stability is lost for every M.A.C. length it is ahead of the CG. A pusher propeller is stabilizing by the same percentage, a plus, since most ultralights are pushers.

One other point worth mentioning is that a windmilling propeller (i.e., one turning by the force of the wind) will shift the aft C.G. limit rearward, compared to a power on situation. If the propeller is stopped, the aerodynamic center will shift rearward even more.

Effect of Center of Gravity Location

As soon as a horizontal tail is added to a wing, the aerodynamic center is moved behind what it was for the wing alone—it is referred to as the aircraft's "neutral

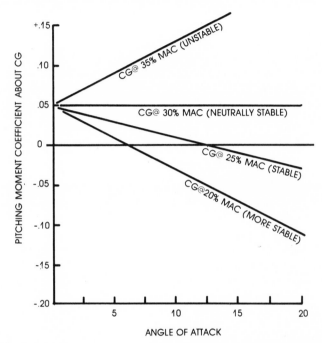

Fig. 9-7. Effect of CG location on pitching moment slope (stability). Neutral point is at 30% M.A.C.

point" (NP). If the CG is placed at the neutral point the aircraft will be neutrally stable. Any CG movement aft the neutral point results in an unstable airplane. Knowing the neutral point, the stability (pitching moment versus angle of attack) for any CG location can be found. In fact, the slope of the pitching moment coefficient versus angle of attack is numerically equal to the distance between the CG and the neutral point, divided by the mean aerodynamic chord. This number is also referred to as the "static margin." The greater the distance between the CG and the NP the higher the static margin and the more stable the aircraft. The larger the static margin, the larger the horizontal tail must be to balance the larger nose down pitching moment.

The vertical position of the CG with respect to the NP also affects an airplane's stability. Moving the CG down—i.e., changing to a high wing configuration—adds to stability. The CG's new moment arm with respect to the NP gives an added nose-down pitching moment with increasing angles of attack. You can think of it as a "pendulum stability" effect. If the CG is moved above the NP, as in a low-wing design, the effect is a decreasing nose-down pitching moment with increasing angle of attack or, instability.

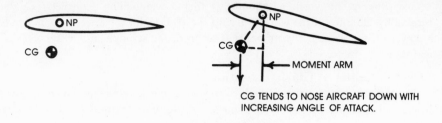

CG TENDS TO NOSE AIRCRAFT DOWN WITH
INCREASING ANGLE OF ATTACK.

CG BELOW NP — ADDED STABILITY (PENDULUM STABILITY)

CRUISING — LOW ANGLE OF ATTACK   SLOW FLIGHT — HIGH ANGLE OF ATTACK

NP COINCIDENT WITH CG (NEUTRAL STABILITY)

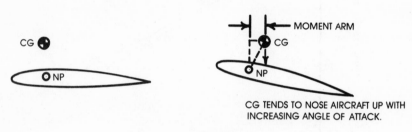

CG TENDS TO NOSE AIRCRAFT UP WITH
INCREASING ANGLE OF ATTACK.

CG ABOVE NP — DESTABILIZING

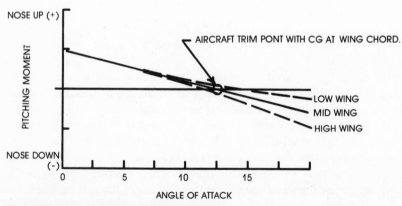

Fig. 9-8. Effect of vertical location of CG on stability.

The Center of Gravity Limits

Unless an ultralight is designed with its center of gravity in line with the pilot's seat, the CG will change with varying pilot weights. If the seat is very near the CG, the aircraft may be able to handle a wide weight range without becoming unstable or uncontrollable. If the seat is far enough away from the CG however, then ballast will need to be added to bring the CG into an area of stability. What this means is that the "center of gravity limit" must be complied with. Typically, a few

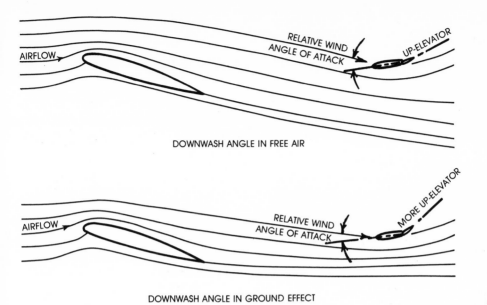

DOWNWASH ANGLE IN FREE AIR

DOWNWASH ANGLE IN GROUND EFFECT

Fig. 9-9. Ground effect reduces downwash angle, requiring move up-elevator to produce $C_L$max.

key points or conditions are calculated and tested to ensure a safe aircraft. Assuming a fuel tank location at the CG, (that way fuel burn off doesn't affect the CG), the only concern we have is the pilot's weight. In an ultralight where the pilot is ahead of the CG, light pilots would mean an aft CG location while heavier pilots would bring it forward. In the case of a light pilot, ballast may have to be added to the nose in order to bring the CG within the stability region. For the heavier pilot, he will obviously make the aircraft more stable, but the maximum weight allowed is determined by control and trim considerations. Many ultralights have adjustable seats to compensate for different pilot weights.

The most forward center of gravity permissible is determined basically by the

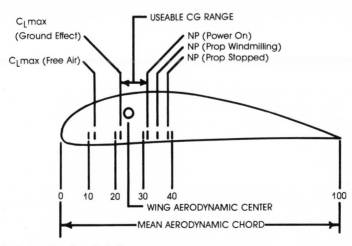

Fig. 9-10. Typical center of gravity limits.

elevator's ability to balance out the airplane's maximum coefficient of lift. This means that our airplane must have:

1) More than adequate horizontal tail authority to rotate for takeoff—tri-geared designs will be able to lift the nosewheel off the ground below stall speed.

2) Enough elevator power to land. If an airplane is loaded in front of its most forward center of gravity position, maximum lift will not be attained with full up elevator. The landing requirement is the largest and it "designs" the elevator and horizontal tail.

At this point it is important to mention that the ground effect experienced during the landing flare actually determines the amount of elevator power required to achieve C_1 max. The ground effect, as mentioned previously, reduces the downward angle behind the wing, putting the tail at a less negative angle of attack with an attendant reduction in tail lift. This situation can only be overcome by increased tail effectiveness either by a larger area or a larger elevator up deflection.

In summary then, the power-on neutral point will determine the aftermost center of gravity location which is of primary importance to stability. The forward-most center of gravity position is determined by the elevator power available in ground effect. Between these two points is the region known as the "static margin" which, as a rule, has no less than 10% of the mean aerodynamic chord between the stick-fixed neutral point and forward center of gravity.

Stick-Free Stability

During the previous discussion, the static longitudinal stability was based on the pilot's feel of the controls as he changed elevator positions to vary the airspeed. It was assumed that the pilot has a hold on the stick at all times, effectively locking the controls. This allowed us to develop the basic stability criterion of pitching moment versus angle of attack, which is actually referred to as stick-fixed static longitudinal stability.

Another way for a pilot to sense an aircraft's stability is by the feel of the force required to move the stick in order to change the airspeed from the trim

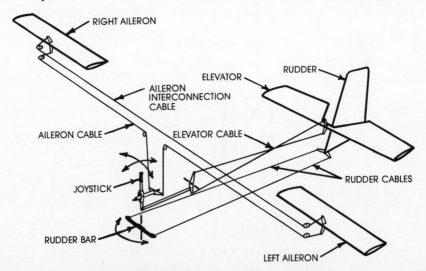

Fig. 9-11. The standard cable operated three-axis aerodynamic control system.

144

condition. The amount of stick force required cannot be directly correlated to the change in pitching moment with angle of attack, but it does relate to another condition—the manner in which pitching moment varies with the stick free. A stable airplane requires a pull force on the stick to fly at speeds below trim, a push force to fly at speeds above trim.

When the stick is let go, the elevator is free to float up as the angle of attack is increased, diminishing the stability from its stick-fixed case. If the elevator is hinged by its leading edge, the float-up actually moves the neutral point forward between 4% to 7% of the mean aerodynamic chord, narrowing the useful center of

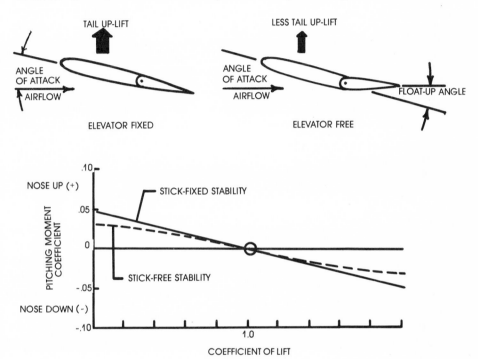

Fig. 9-12. Releasing hold of the stick allows the elevator to float-up, reducing stability.

gravity range. Naturally, the stick is held most of the time so stick-free stability only becomes a concern when the aircraft is flown "hands-off." If it can be flown hands-off for a period of time, it probably has adequate stability.

An airplane would be neutrally stable stick-free if the elevator float-up angle was equal to the elevator angle required for trim, and the pilot would not need to apply any force to the stick at any other than the original trim speed. An airplane would be called stick-free unstable if the elevator float-up angle exceeds that required for an angle of attack above the original trim angle, and the pilot would have to push forward on the stick. And finally, an airplane is considered stick-free stable if the elevator float-up angle is less than that required to hold an angle of attack above the original trim condition, and the pilot would have to pull back on the stick.

The above may seem elementary, but there was a time when airplane builders argued which direction the stick should be moved to change airspeed from trim.

145

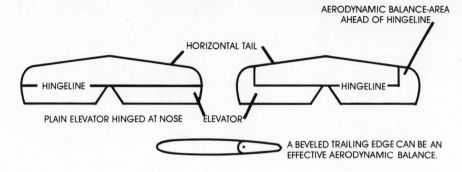

Fig. 9-13. Two basic types of elevators — plain and aerodynamically balanced.

Incidentally, rudder control was also argued—should it be like a sled's steering bar, or a push in the desired direction? But that's all been resolved since then, the result being the standard, or Deperdussin, type three axis control system.

Augmenting Low Stick Forces

If the aerodynamically induced stick forces are not great enough to give a nice feel to the aircraft's stick, or to overcome the friction band, several methods can be

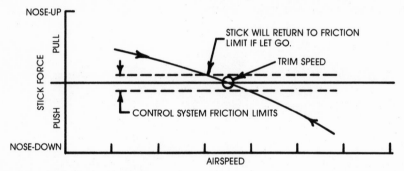

Fig. 9-14. How stick-forces vary with airspeed.

employed to alter that feel, thereby increasing the stick-free stability. Low stick forces can be increased by adding a "downspring" or a bobweight to the stick. The spring could be in simple tension, or in a spiral (as with clockwork springs) for constant force. The bobweight is simply a mass of metal hung on the

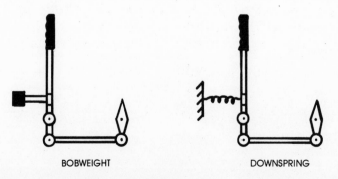

Fig. 9-15. Artificial methods of improving control "feel".

stick that pulls the stick forward with a constant force. The bobweight also has the added effect of responding to accelerations. If an up gust hits the airplane, the bobweight's inertia will pull the stick forward, helping to lower the nose. Also, during a turn, the bobweight pulls the stick forward giving the pilot an extra desire to haul back on the stick—as he, of course, should.

The Maneuvering Points

While ultralights spend the larger part of their flying time in straight and level unaccelerated flight, they are required to do a lot of maneuvering. This means they must possess adequate stability and control to fly in curved flight paths.

In straight and level unaccelerated flight, the four main forces are balanced in static equilibrium. As soon as a turn or other curved flight path is entered however, the equilibrium is upset and an unbalanced force develops perpendicular to the flight path, causing the aircraft to curve. The simplest example of this would be a sharp pull-up. Here, the pilot hauls back on the stick too fast for the aircraft to slow down, thereby generating a lift force that exceeds the gross weight. Turning an aircraft is also the result of an unbalanced force perpendicular to the flight path. In this case, the aircraft lift vector is tilted off the vertical, requiring it to be larger than in level unaccelerated flight, if its vertical component is to balance the gross weight. Forces generated in both the turn and the pull-up are felt in the seat of the pants as excess body weight—in other words, g-loads.

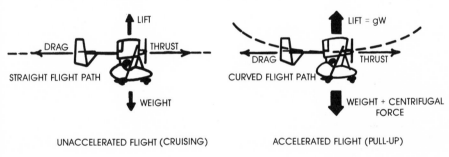

Fig. 9-16. The four main forces are balanced in unaccelerated flight, and unbalanced in accelerated flight.

The turn and pull-up maneuvers just described involve motions about the pitch axis, which are somewhat dampened by the horizontal tail. This requires increased up elevator and more pull on the stick to overcome the aircraft's stability. The pitch damping actually induces greater stability over the static case, in effect pushing the stick-fixed and stick-free neutral points aft. The CG where the elevator angle required to accelerate the aircraft into a curved flight path is zero,

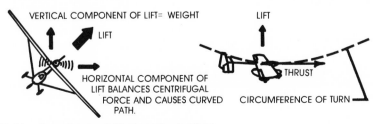

Fig. 9-17. A turn in another example of accelerated flight.

147

is called the stick-fixed maneuver point. The CG where the stick force required to accelerate the aircraft is zero is called the stick-free maneuver point. In other words, shifting the CG back creates the necessary pitching moments to go into a curved flight path, completely overriding the need of an elevator. Needless to say, the pilot would be helpless if his aircraft were balanced at the so-called maneuver points. The maneuver points could be reached by a light pilot in an ultralight that has the pilot in front of the CG. He would have to carry ballast in the nose to get the CG forward of the maneuver points.

Elevator Angle Per g

As curved path accelerated flight is increased, the elevator angle required to maintain a given coefficient of lift is also increased. This is due to the damping moments generated by the rotation about the pitch axis which generates an additional angle of attack on the bottom of the tail, reducing the tail down lift.

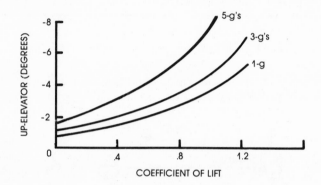

Fig. 9-18. Up-elevator deflection increases with g-loads in a pull-up.

For an elevator to be effective it must have enough power to accelerate the aircraft to stall, which should occur before something breaks! The farther forward the CG, the larger the elevator power required to do this, which imposes a new limit on the forward CG based on g-loads. As it turns out however, the elevator angle required to develop $C_L$max in ground effect during landing is the stiffer requirement regarding forward CG, and it determines the elevator design, as mentioned previously.

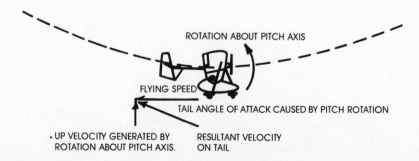

Fig. 9-19. Tail negative angle of attack is increased in curved flight path, requiring still more up-elevator to hold C_L.

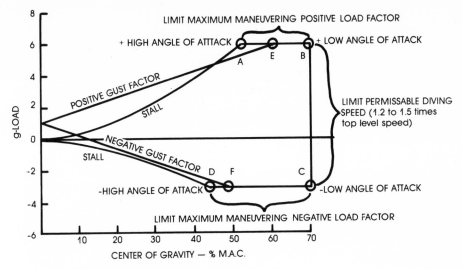

Fig. 9-20. The V-g diagram depicts an ultralight's flight envelope.

Stick Force Per g

The most important criterion regarding an airplane's feel is the amount of stick force required to maneuver. In other words, the stick force needed to produce a one-g acceleration—the stick force per g—is primarily what gives an airplane its feel. Over the years, it has been well accepted that the pilot's feeling of an aircraft's maneuvering abilities is directly related to the stick force gradient versus g-load. Designers should strive to stay within certain gradient limits in order to produce an aircraft with nice handling qualities. Furthermore, the gradient varies directly with the CG getting lighter as the CG moves back toward the stick-free maneuver point, where it is zero. An aircraft with its CG at the stick-free maneuver point would be extremely dangerous to fly. Any small movement of the stick would result in the airplane going into an extremely violent divergent maneuver and possibly loading the airframe to the point of structural failure before any thing could be done about it. Too low a stick force gradient and an airplane's handling becomes too sensitive and prone to high g-load producing maneuvers. Too high a gradient and the airplanes becomes tiring to fly.

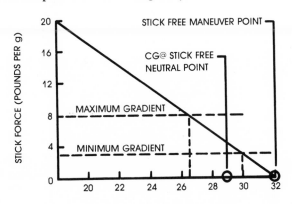

Fig. 9-21. Stick force gradient range as established for fighter aircraft.

149

During WWII the Army and Navy established limits to the stick force per g for various kinds of airplanes. They found that for fighters the range between 3 and 8 pounds per g was acceptable, while bombers could have an upper limit of around 35 pounds per g. These limits had the affect of limiting the CG range even more. The maximum gradient establishing the forward CG, while the minimum gradient set the aft CG.

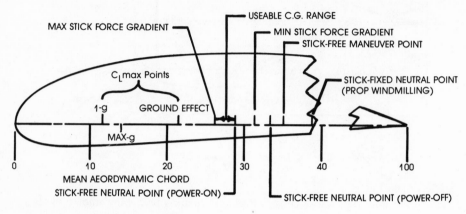

Fig. 9-22. The various limits on an airplane's center of gravity.

Final Limits on An Airplane's Center of Gravity

To sum up our discussion of static longitudinal stability and control, let's construct a diagram depicting the important CG points on a mean aerodynamic chord. Examining this we see that the useable CG range is actually very small. It is the designer's task to make it as broad as possible, and the pilot's responsibility to load his aircraft properly to be within the designer's specified range.

Longitudinal Dynamics

Longitudinal dyanmics basically involves the response of an aircraft to a disturbance from equilibrium flight and the interim motions of the aircraft in its response to pilot control inputs. The study of longitudinal dynamics is important in determining the control required to fly an airplane and the pilot's ability to react to control needs.

There are two characteristic modes of motion for the stick-fixed longitudinal case, a heavily damped short period oscillation and a lightly damped long period oscillation called the "phugoid." The short period mode is so fast and so heavily damped by the horizontal tail, that it can hardly be noticed and is of virtually no concern to an ultralight pilot. The phugoid mode can possibly be experienced by trimming the aircraft for straight and level flight, then "freezing" the stick into a fixed position. After a while, the phugoid will develop as evidenced by a gradual roller-coaster type flight path in which airspeed and altitude are traded off in an exchange of kinetic and potential energy. Fortunately, the period of the phugoid is so long that it does not affect the flying qualities of the aircraft. Furthermore, in lightly loaded aircraft such as ultralights, the two modes tend to merge together in their periods. In other words, ultralight pilots really don't need to concern themselves with either one.

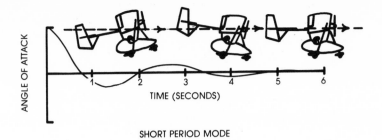

SHORT PERIOD MODE

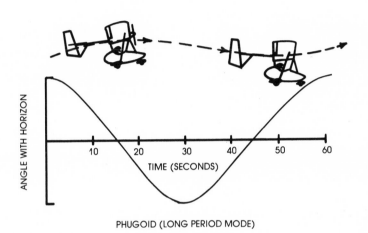

PHUGOID (LONG PERIOD MODE)

Fig. 9-23. The two longitudinal dynamic modes.

When we consider the stick-free longitudinal dynamic case, we again encounter two modes—a long and a short. The short period stick-free mode, like the short period stick-free mode—the so-called "porpoising" mode—however, is another story, period stick-free mode—the so-called "porpoising" mode—lowever, is another story but only for heavy aircraft. The trouble with the porpoising mode is that its period is not long enough and its damping weak enough, so that the pilot must concern himself with it at all times. But ultralighters need not worry about this one.

There's another porpoising mode that the ultralight pilot does need to be aware of, but only with canards aircraft. It's a stick-fixed mode of medium period that manifests itself with full aft stick during slow flight. It develops when the canard (here meaning the small, forward wing) which could be carrying 20% of the aircraft's gross weight, has stalled, drops, unstalls, rises, stalls, and so on... while the main wing remains flying. This is characteristic of a properly set up canard, and has the advantage of practically eliminating the total stall and fall of the aircraft—a tremendous safety feature.

151

Chapter Ten

Directional Stability and Control

Directional stability and control concern the movements of an aircraft outside the plane of symmetry. In other words, it has to do with whether or not the aircraft is flying in the direction it is headed (i.e., pointing towards)! More specifically, it deals with aircraft motions and orientations that produce a relative wind on the side of the aircraft—an angle of sideslip. In general, a sideslip angle does nothing good for an airplane, except to increase drag in some tight landing situations as a method for steepening the landing approach, during one-engine-out situations for twins, and as an aid to certain aerobatic maneuvers.

Proper directional stability and control is necessary for an airplane to maintain equilibrium at zero sideslip, and to enable the pilot to control the aircraft so as to direct it into zero sideslip during maneuvers and winds that cause sideslip. When zero sideslip is easily maintained, pilots enjoy the aircraft's handling qualities.

At this point, it is important to mention the difference between sideslip and yaw. Sideslip, as mentioned above, is the angle the relative wind makes with the centerline of the aircraft. Yaw, on the other hand, is the angular movement of the aircraft's centerline from a particular direction at some point in time. A coordinated

90 degree turn, for example, means the airplane yawed 90 degrees with no sideslip. During a straight slip, as used in an approach to landing, the angle of sideslip is equal but opposite to the angle of yaw.

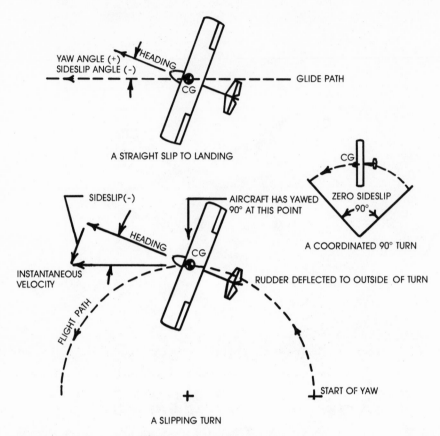

Fig. 10-1. The differences between sideslip and yaw.

Static Directional Stability

Static directional stability is commonly expressed as an aircraft's characteristic tendency to develop yawing moments that tend to restore it to its original equilibrium trim condition, which is normally zero sideslip. Similar to the longitudinal case, directional stability can be related to a yawing moment coefficient versus angle of yaw. For stability, the yawing moment must grow increasingly negative as the yaw angle increases.

The vertical tail is the main contributor to yaw stability. The moment it creates is simply its lift times the distance of its aerodynamic center from the airplane's center of gravity. While vertical tails are generally of a low geometric aspect ratio, their effective aspect is about 155% times the geometric because of the end plate effect of the horizontal tail. Verticals simply don't need a high aspect, because 99% of the time they are in zero sideslip where they produce no side lift and therefore no induced drag.

The wing also contributes to yaw stability, but just slightly. It is somewhat significant though for sweptback wings, while sweptforward wings are destabilizing.

Straight wings contribute virtually nothing to the yaw stability. Each ten degrees of sweepback is equivalent to about one degree of dihedral, the effect increasing the higher the coefficient of lift. This can be dangerous, as increased dihedral leads to "Dutch Roll" instability which we will discuss shortly.

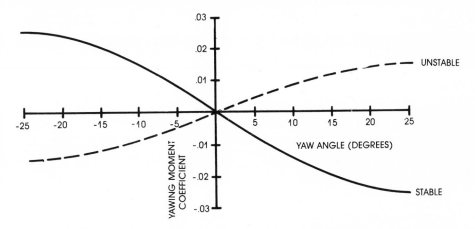

Fig. 10-2. A wind tunnel plot of yawing moment coefficient versus angle of yaw.

Several items detract from yaw stability, like fuselages and nacelles, but these are mostly absent on ultralights. Rotating propellers are destabilizing as tractors, but stabilizing as pushers—a plus for many ultralights. Floats added to an otherwise wheeled ultralight are definitely destabilizing and require a larger vertical stabilizer to compensate. Center of gravity movements have virtually no effect on directional stability, however.

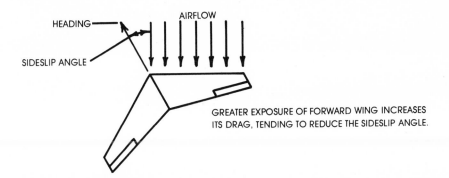

Fig. 10-3. A sweptback wing contributes to yaw stability.

In terms of handling qualities, the more directional stability an aircraft has, the better it handles and the more pilots like it.

Directional Control

The rudder, which is used to control yaw (it is not used to produce a turn), was born out of the need to correct the imperfect turn created when the Wright brothers warped the wings of their gliders for roll. Up until the time they discovered the need to make their fixed vertical surfaces moveable, they had been

PONTOONS INCREASE THE VERTICAL TAIL AREA REQUIRED FOR DIRECTIONAL STABILITY.

Fig. 10-4. The vertical tail is the primary determinant of directional stability.

flying only with pitch and roll control. Trouble was, when a roll was initiated at low speeds, the glider would yaw in the direction opposite the intended turn. This was the first case of what is now known as adverse aileron yaw. Here's how it works.

For instance, let's say Orville wants to make a left turn. He'd move his hip cradle to the left, warping the right wing tip trailing edge down and the left wing tip trailing edge up. The right wing generated more lift and the left wing less, resulting in a roll to the left and a yaw to the right. The problem was created because while the right wing generated more lift, it also generated more induced drag, tending to yaw the glider right. In a flash of inspiration, the brother solved the problem by hinging the vertical fin and connecting it to the warp control so that it deflected in the intended direction of turn. In other words, the rudder was created *solely* to counterbalance the adverse yaw caused by the wing warping. (It is interesting to note that the early European flyers, ignorant of the secret of roll control, continued to make—when they made them at all—wide skidding turns for several years after the Wright Brothers' first flights.)

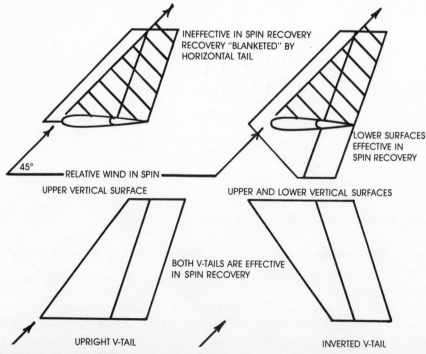

Fig. 10-5. How various vertical tails affect spin recovery.

As mentioned already, the rudder is quite useful to balance adverse yaw when it exists, particularly at high coefficients of lift. If the aircraft's roll control system is properly designed however, adverse yaw should not exist. Differential ailerons (the up aileron goes up more than the down aileron goes down), or spoilers can accomplish this.

Another reason for rudders is in controlling the yaw caused by slipstream rotation, which is particularly powerful under high power, low airspeed conditions. The air blown back by the propeller is given a slight rotation, causing it to strike the vertical tail on one side, thereby generating a yawing moment.

The third reason for employing a rudder is to perform crosswing takeoffs and landings up to 80% of the stalling speed.

The fourth reason for including a rudder is to control spins, though a noble design goal is a non-spinnable airplane.

The final reason for installing a rudder is to counterbalance the sideslip caused when one engine goes out on a twin. This criterion normally "designs" the size of the rudder.

HUMMER (UPRIGHT V)

LAZAIR (INVERTED V)

Fig. 10-6. Two examples of ultralights with V-tails.

If an ultralight can be designed with a high degree of directional stability, a tricycle landing gear (for ground stability, because taildraggers are unstable as explained in Chapter Fourteen), no slipstream over the vertical tail, no tendency to spin, and a single engine, it shouldn't need a rudder at all. After all, birds and Rogallo hang gliders do very well without them, and 99% of most flights can be made without using rudder period.

Pilots prefer rudder pedals that require a reasonable push before they say an airplane handles nicely directionally. If the push force needed to control sideslip is too low, pilots feel uneasy about the airplane. A rudder normally constitutes about 50% of the total vertical tail surface area.

V-Tails

Instead of the standard single vertical tail, several ultralights incorporate the so-called V-tail. Whether upright or inverted, the V-tail offers two surfaces in place of three, and excellent spin recovery characteristics. V-tails usually have the propeller blowing between them, so they aren't subject to the rotating slipstream. The inverted V-tail offers the added advantage of a favorable rolling moment with rudder control inputs, as does any underslung vertical tail. (A top mounted rudder actually produces a roll in the direction opposite the intended yaw.)

V-tails offer some disadvantages, as well. They require a somewhat complicated mixer mechanism to allow the moveable surfaces to function as both elevator and rudder. They also respond to both horizontal and vertical gusts, which can lead to "hunting," an oscillation about the yaw and pitch axes, that can cause nausea while flying in turbulence for any length of time. But once again, inverted V-tails are superior to upright V-tails because they tend to roll the aircraft in the direction of yaw.

T-Tails

T-tails (the horizontal stabilizer is mounted on top of the vertical fin) have not been extensively employed on ultralights probably because of the extra structural and weight requirements put on the vertical tail and aft fuselage. They do offer excellent spin recovery, but also a more complicated control system. T-tail design can be quite critical. If not located properly, the horizontal tail could enter the wake of the stalled wing and be rendered ineffective, where it might actually lock the aircraft into what is known as a "deep" stall. The stabilizer gets caught in the wake of the wing, and can't get out.

Chapter Eleven
Lateral Stability and Control

During the early days of the modern ultralight, it was quite common to see aircraft with only a two-axis control system—rudder and elevator. While the designers claimed this was perfectly adequate for the intended operational envelope—calm conditions—progress has had something else to say about this. Ultralight pilots are no longer content flying only in the calm of mornings and evenings. They want more air time and are willing to endure crosswinds and light turbulence to get it. Then, too, as more and more licensed pilots get into ultralights, their prior flight experience made them want a more positive form of roll control. Hence, the re-appearance of the three-axis control system as invented by the Wrights in 1902!

As described previously, an airplane is turned by rolling its lift vector off the vertical, i.e., by banking. This can be accomplished, to a degree, without ailerons or spoilers, but leaves something to be desired. A turn in a two-axis, rudder and elevator ultralight is actually the result of a sideslip. The rudder is deflected in the desired direction, the aircraft yaws, then sideslips. If the wing has enough effective dihedral, the skid velocity will increase the angle of attack, and therefore the lift of the outside wing, generating a net rolling moment away from the skid, banking the airplane. This event is due to dihedral effect, but it is too weak for flight in almost any crosswind. Besides which, the aircraft must skid sideways for this to work, which is dangerous near the ground.

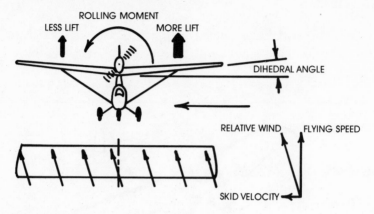

Fig. 11-1. How dihedral produces a rolling moment in a skid.

Dutch Roll

For dihedral effect to produce a coordinated turn, it must have the cooperation of the vertical tail. If the tail is just the right size, it'll happen. If the tail is too small and the dihedral too large, the aircraft will have a tendency to "Dutch Roll" in response to side gusts or rudder deflections. This would be the typical scenario: Let's say the aircraft is hit by a sharp gust from the left. It responds by skidding to the right and yawing to the left, into the gust. The right wing now has more speed than the left wing, so it develops more lift and induced drag causing it to roll left and yaw right. The now raised right wing causes a slip to the left. This picks up the left wing, causing a right roll and a left yaw. The vertical tail reacts to left slip due to its "weathercocking" tendency, and aids the left yaw. The right wing moves forward developing more lift and induced drag causing a left roll and a right yaw. Now the vertical tail reacts and continues the right yaw, and the aircraft begins slipping left. And so on...the term Dutch Roll comes from the motion made by Dutch ice skaters. It's basically a slow oscillation in roll of between 5 to 15 degrees coupled to a yawing oscillation of 5 to 10 degrees to both sides of the flight path. The Dutch roll can be catastrophic. If the oscillations continue to grow, they could send the aircraft into a barrel roll. It can probably be cured by the increase in vertical tail area that is needed anyway to head the aircraft into slips as soon as they start.

Spiral Dive

At the other end of the stick is the case of too large a vertical fin and not enough dihedral. In a slip, the vertical fin simply takes control and heads the airplane into the slip, while the low dihedral can't generate a compensating roll. Without holding up the nose, the aircraft will begin losing altitude in the direction of the slip. The airspeed will increase while the aircraft continues to turn in a decreasing slip, increasing the airspeed still further, and so forth. The phenomenon is known as spiral instability.

Most aircraft exhibit some spiral instability, but it is of such a large radius that it goes unnoticed. An aircraft can be made completely auto stable, such as a free flight model airplane, but the excess stability hinders controllability, so a slight spiral instability is actually desirable under most flight conditions. Spiral instability is not desirable however, if you get into a cloud. It is virtually impossible to fly straight and level on only airspeed, ball and yaw string.

Any ultralight that becomes popular with the public will undoubtedly lie somewhere between being spirally unstable and exhibiting Dutch Roll. Spiral stability can be improved by increasing dihedral and/or reducing the size of the vertical tail. Dutch Roll can be decreased by adding to the vertical tail and/or decreasing dihedral. Too much dihedral makes crosswind operations more difficult, requiring increased slipping to make up for the tendency of the wing to be rolled away from the wind. This also means that since more aileron is required to counteract a crosswind, the amount of roll control diminishes with increasing dihedral.

From a handling point of view, pilots prefer an airplane with plenty of roll authority. There should still be some aileron available at the greatest slip angle possible, which implies the rudder's effectiveness should drop off first. And once again, we can say that some stability is desirable while too much detracts from controllability, requiring the pilot to "fight" the airplane constantly.

Lateral Control Surfaces

The modern ultralight airplane typically incorporates some form of lateral control device in, on, or near the wing. Whereas, more conventional aircraft normally employ ailerons, ultralights also use externally mounted ailerons, wing tip draggers and spoilers. All serve the function of producing a rolling moment about the aircraft's longitudinal axis, and each has its usefulness.

AILERONS DEFLECTED FOR A LEFT
BANK ALTER LIFT DISTRIBUTION,
DEVELOPING A LEFT ROLLING
MOMENT.

Fig. 11-2. Deflected ailerons alter the lift distribution for roll.

Ailerons

Ailerons in their basic form are simply plain flaps hinged at their leading edges, located in the trailing edge of the outer wing panels. When actuated they deflect asymmetrically, one goes up while the other goes down, changing the local wing camber and the total lift distribution across the wing. An aircraft rolls in the direction of the up aileron. That aileron reduces the local camber and lift while the down aileron increases the local camber and lift—the net effect being a rolling moment.

As soon as an aircraft begins rolling however, the rolling velocity creates a lift distribution of its own, opposing or damping the originally intended roll. This happens because the wing's rolling velocity changes the angle of attack all across the wing, the angle getting larger (plus and minus) as the tip is approached. The damping moments are considerable, particularly at ultralight speeds, and point out the need for really effective ailerons.

For ailerons to be effective on an ultralight, they need to be large. The design of good ailerons is not easy since pilots like them to feel relatively light, while their actuation requires sideways stick pressure, the direction in which the human arm is weakest. Flight near the stall speed is what sizes an aileron, which must be large enough to pick up a wing, particularly during final approach. High speed flight is concerned more with the stick forces required, which may necessitate aerodynamic balancing to assist the pilot of conventional airplanes but not in ultralights. Roll control effectiveness is typically quoted as the time, in seconds, it takes to roll from 45 degrees in one direction to 45 degrees in the other (4 seconds would be good). Ailerons are also used to counteract dihedral in a sideslip, during crabbing flight and for balance during an engine-out situation on a twin.

Like a wing, an aileron should have a moderate aspect ratio to be most effective. Wide chord, short span ailerons have no place on any airplane, because they just don't produce as much change in the local wing lift distribution, and therefore less of a rolling moment.

Over the years, it has been proven that pilots relate lateral control effectiveness not so much to the rate of roll, as they do to the helix angle the wing tips make during the roll. (In other words, the slower you fly the slower your roll rate needs to be. The helix angle remains relatively constant.) This angle is determined by multiplying the roll rate (p) in degrees per second, times the wingspan (b), in feet, divided by the airspeed (V) in miles per hour or, pb/V which would be equal to about 15 for an ultralight at full aileron deflection. This relationship normally will size an aileron, and is a constant up to some speed where the wing's elasticity allows the tips to twist opposite the aileron deflection, thus slowing the roll. At some speed, the wing will twist enough to completely cancel the rolling moment. That is why some lightly built ultralights employ spoilers (see page 164). They won't cause a wing to twist.

The longer a wing for a given wing area, and the further away the aileron is from its center, the greater the aileron power. Trouble is, the increased span also raises

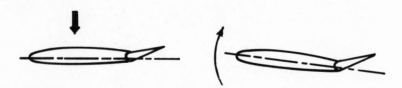

A RIGID WING WITH UP AILERON WILL DROP   AN ELASTIC WING WITH UP AILERON WILL TWIST

Fig. 11-3. At higher speeds the elasticity of a wing will allow it to twist, due to a deflected aileron, negating the intended roll.

the roll damping—long wings just don't like high roll rates. Taper ratio is important, too. A tapered wing will roll faster than a rectangular wing. Once again, as in all aspects of airplane design, aileron design is a compromise.

Where higher speeds are approached, say above 50 mph, aileron flutter could also be a consideration. To prevent this wild oscillation of the ailerons, they need to be statically balanced about their hinge line, and kept away from the extreme wing tip. The wing tip vortices can induce flutter at a lower speed than it might otherwise occur. That's why ailerons are typically mounted inboard of the tip.

Differential Aileron Deflection

For ailerons to provide the purest roll response, they must operate so as to produce minimum adverse yaw. One method of accomplishing this is through differential ailerons—the up going aileron deflects perhaps three times the angle of the down going aileron. This differential allows the up aileron to compensate for the down aileron's induced drag, which is really the cause of adverse aileron yaw. If adverse yaw exists at all it'll show up at slower speeds, and require help from the

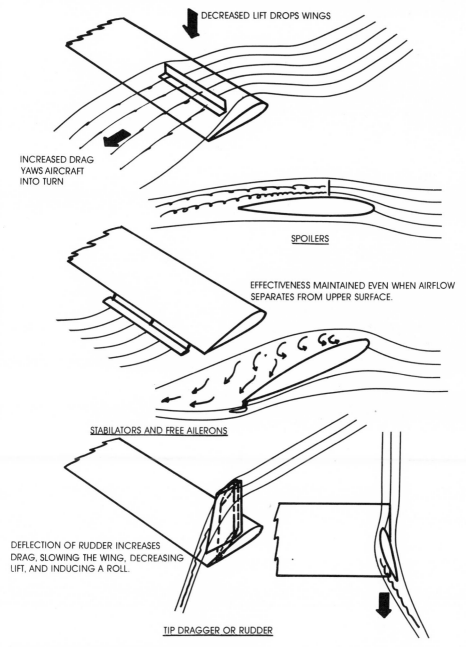

DECREASED LIFT DROPS WINGS

INCREASED DRAG
YAWS AIRCRAFT
INTO TURN

SPOILERS

EFFECTIVENESS MAINTAINED EVEN WHEN AIRFLOW
SEPARATES FROM UPPER SURFACE.

STABILATORS AND FREE AILERONS

DEFLECTION OF RUDDER INCREASES
DRAG, SLOWING THE WING, DECREASING
LIFT, AND INDUCING A ROLL.

TIP DRAGGER OR RUDDER

Fig. 11-4. Various alternate forms of roll control devices.

rudder to prevent sideslipping. If an ultralight is highly directionally stable and has a low effective dihedral, it is easier to coordinate turns. It also rolls the fastest because it doesn't need rudder to counteract adverse yaw.

Aileron Control Forces

The aileron control forces of an ultralight should be on the order of one-half to two pounds or so, not counting control system friction. The lower the friction the better the aileron feel to the pilot.

Aileron Control Function

To clarify any confusion that may exist concerning how ailerons are used, be aware that they are rate controls. In other words, they are deflected to *initiate* a roll. Once the desired bank angle is achieved, they are either neutralized or perhaps even reversed. The need to reverse them to prevent over-banking is of concern at slower speed, smaller radius turns where the outer wing panel has more speed and lift than the inner panel. Normal cruising speeds and larger radius turns however, will reduce or eliminate the need to reverse stick once a bank is established.

OTHER FORMS OF ROLL CONTROL

There are some alternatives to ailerons for roll control, and ultralights have been pioneered in this area. You'll find spoilers, stabilators, free ailerons, and tip draggers used on various designs.

Spoilers

A spoiler is basically a rectangular flat plate that normally lies flush with the upper surface of the outer wing. When actuated, it moves up out of the boundary layer as much as 90 degrees, disrupting the airflow—reducing lift and increasing drag. Used one at a time, they produce roll and yaw, and if properly designed can produce coordinated turns. Deflected simultaneously, they allow precise glide path control—full deflection of both can get you into a small landing area in a hurry because of the steep glide angle.

Since only one spoiler is used for a roll, it must be larger than an aileron to be just as effective, in fact, it must be about one and one-half to two times the span of an aileron. Besides that, placement is very important. The further forward the spoiler, the larger percentage of the lift it spoils, but the slower the response to actuation. When they take effect though, look out! Spoilers are typically located aft the mid-chord point and have chords of about ten percent of the local wing chord. This location and size allows the roll to occur more in time with when the spoilers are deflected.

Spoilers do not feel exactly like ailerons. They exhibit a favorable yaw, i.e., into the intended roll, but they cannot pick up a wing, per se—they can only drop a wing. But then again, since they don't increase camber as a down going aileron does, there's little chance they'll cause the high wing to stall, and so reduce the risk of a spin.

Stabilators and Free Ailerons

Stabilators and free ailerons are actually auxiliary wings mounted below the outer trailing edge of a wing, one per panel. In the case of the stabilator, they are used both for pitch as well as roll control. Simultaneous deflections in one direction control pitch, while assymetric deflections produce rolling moments. Free ailerons, of course, deflect opposite and are used only for roll.

The advantage of stabilators and free ailerons is that they are always flying in the energy laden, attached airflow beneath the wing providing control response even at the stall. The disadvantage of these surfaces is that they also increase drag over what would be for flush mounted ailerons. They must be properly balanced to avoid flutter.

Tip Draggers

Tip draggers, or rudders, were pioneered on ultralights as a simple method of lateral control. They are mounted at the wing tip, and extend perpendicular to the wing. Deflection of one produces yaw and roll, while both can be deflected for glide path control.

Control Surface Design

The horizontal and vertical tail surfaces, referred to collectively as the empennage, are essential for the stability and control of a conventional design. They are typically of a lower aspect ratio than the wing—remember low aspect ratios stall at a higher angle of attack—helping to ensure that they "fly" as the wing stalls.

In general, it is desirable to have fairly thin airfoil sections for the tail surfaces. (Flat tail surfaces are inferior to airfoiled ones). This is no problem for externally braced surfaces, but cantilevered tails require spar depth for strength and will probably need to be 6 to 9% thick. Thinness is important not only to minimize drag, but for reasons of control effectiveness as well. Thicker airfoils suffer from larger wakes, establishing an area near the neutral position that renders the rudder and elevator ineffective. Deflections inside the wake don't have any affect, and the control surfaces are unable to center solidly. Poor centering may even cause porpoising.

Chapter Twelve

Unconventional Configurations

The Canard

Canards are in vogue today, but they are nothing new—the Wright brothers' Kitty Hawk Flyer was a canard. It is important to understand that a canard is not a conventional airplane with the horizontal stabilizer simply moved to the nose. The old concept of a canard being a "tail first" airplane is incorrect, since any lifting surface in front of the center of gravity detracts from longitudinal stability. In order for a pitch disturbance in any airplane to be corrected, the natural aerodynamic restoring forces can only be provided by a lifting surface *behind* the center of gravity. Thus, in a canard, the main wing (behind the center of gravity) actually becomes the horizontal stabilizer.

Static longitudinal stability can be gauged by what is termed "tail volume coefficient," a product of stabilizer area times its distance from the center of gravity divided by the wing area times the mean aerodynamic chord. For a canard, the tail volume coefficient of the front surface must be subtracted from the tail volume coefficient of the wing. In the case of successful canards, the net aft center of

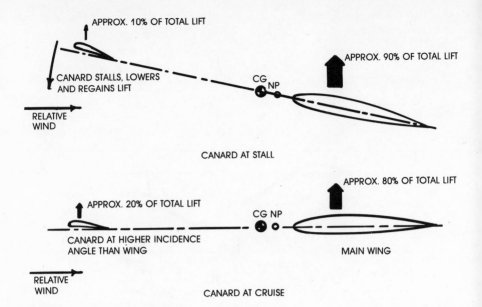

APPROX. 10% OF TOTAL LIFT

CANARD STALLS, LOWERS
AND REGAINS LIFT

APPROX. 90% OF TOTAL LIFT

CG NP

RELATIVE
WIND

CANARD AT STALL

APPROX. 20% OF TOTAL LIFT

CANARD AT HIGHER INCIDENCE
ANGLE THAN WING

APPROX. 80% OF TOTAL LIFT

CG NP

MAIN WING

RELATIVE
WIND

CANARD AT CRUISE

Fig. 12-1. Basic arrangement for logitudinal stability in a canard.

gravity tail volume coefficient is more than adequate for proper static longitudinal stability.

Contributions to the dynamic pitch stability can stem only from lifting surfaces configured ahead and aft the center of gravity. For conventionals, dynamic longitudinal stability is determined primarily by the horizontal stabilizer, with no significant contributions from the wing. The canard, on the other hand, benefits in dynamic pitch stability from both the main and forward surfaces. As the stall is approached, instead of the aircraft falling out of the air, the canard itself stalls before the main wing. As soon as the canard stalls, the nose comes down slightly and lift is restored. If the stick is held back, the canard goes from stalled to unstalled in a characteristic short period "bobbing" motion, while the aircraft continues to fly unstalled, as mentioned previously.

For a canard to be inherently stable and to the pilot's liking, it must meet the following criteria:

a) The rate of change of pitching moment with respect to center of gravity must be higher for the main wing than for the canard.

b) The canard must stall before the main wing has reached its maximum lift.

c) The canard and main wing must have a minimum incidence difference, i.e., zero lift direction difference, that cannot be lowered by the canard elevator or any other flap.

To attain these goals, successful canards have several things in common: 1) A high aspect ratio canard with a lift curve slope steeper than the main wing set at a higher incidence angle than the main wing, to insure its stalls first. 2) A swept back main wing with tip mounted vertical fins and rudders to insure adequate directional stability. The sweepback also aids in producing an adequate static margin for longitudinal stability, as well as balancing a rear mounted engine. The verticals are often winglets for reducing wing tip vortices. 3) The vertical placement of the canard with respect to the main wing is important, since downwash and tip vortices produced by the canard could interfere with the main wing's stall characteristics. This is one area where designers differ, flight testing giving the ultimate answer for each configuration. 4) Sweepback is not necessary provided a vertical tail or tails can be supported aft the wing. Remember, a sweptback wing is not as efficient as a straight wing.

Properly designed canard airplanes offer the advantage of being virtually unstallable and therefore unspinnable. They can also be more efficient than rear tailed designs, because the canard carries part of the aircraft's weight, whereas the

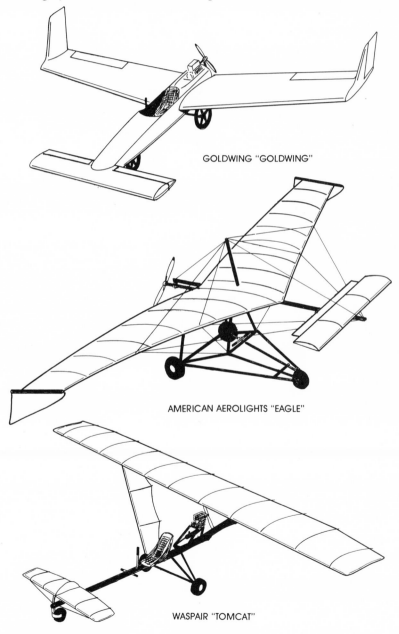

GOLDWING "GOLDWING"

AMERICAN AEROLIGHTS "EAGLE"

WASPAIR "TOMCAT"

Fig. 12-2. Some canard ultralights.

rear tail produces a negative load. This load sharing also means lower structural requirements for each wing.

The direct disadvantages of canards should be considered, as well. Having the canard stall first means that the main wing cannot develop its maximum lift. This means it lands faster, requires a longer runway, and cannot thermal as well as conventional configurations. Furthermore, the canard cannot handle the heavy pitching moment created by wing flaps.

Incidentally, the noun, canard seems to have been chosen from the French verb "canarder" which means "to pitch," in an aerodynamic sense. Ultralights incorporating the canard concept are the Goldwing, Tomcat, and Eagle. Also one of the more ambitious NASA research programs, the HIMAT (Highly Maneuverable Aircraft Technology) is consistently centered around the canard concept.

Flying Wings

The flying wing is perhaps the epitome of the aeronautical engineer's art—a form follows function finale in which everything on the aircraft contributes to lift. Down through the years, flying wings have come and gone, never quite gaining acceptance from pilots. The U.S. government even helped fund development of the "ultimate" bomber, the Northrop XB-35/49 series flying wings during the late 1940's. This 172 foot span, four-engined leviathan had a maximum overload gross weight of 225,000 pounds and a 10,000 mile range, with the jet version topping out at nearly 500 mph. Some say it wasn't steady enough in yaw to serve as a bombing platform (which could be compensated for with an auto stabilization system anyway), but it is also well known that political problems intervened, and the Convair B-36 "Peacemaker" won the roll as our nation's strategic bomber during the 1950's. Nevertheless, the Northrop wings were proven stable and highly maneuverable.

Theoretically, flying wings offer many efficiencies over their more conventional cousins. The total drag can be as little as 50% resulting in a 25% reduction in power required. Maximum range of a flying wing is up to 43% greater for the same cruising speed. Full throttle speeds of a flying wing require as little as 50% power and conversely, the range can be as high as 192% that of conventional types. At comparable power settings, flying wing top speeds are about 25% greater.

At any rate, the flying wing appears to have been finally vindicated by the ultralight world. For the first time in history, a significant number of these all-wing wonders are being produced as ultralights in the form of the Mitchell Aircraft Corporation's models B-10 and U-2.

After reading about tailed aircraft stability previously in this book, you might question a flying wing's stability. Longitudinal stability is a bit more critical than for a tailed or canard configuration, but not excessively so. In the past, various techniques have been employed to bring about a proper stability, among them being: sweepback, a reflexed airfoil, and wingtip washout. An additional technique has been developed by designer Don Mitchell (he once worked for Northrop) who began his ultralight engineering where Northrop left off.

If you try to fly a conventionally cambered wing with the center of gravity ahead of the aerodynamic center to provide longitudinal stability, you'll find that the entire trailing edge must be bent up, leaving the wing with virtually no nose-up control, not to mention a large trim drag. This can be improved upon by using an airfoil that is reflexed (upturned trailing edge), which eliminates the nose down pitching moment.

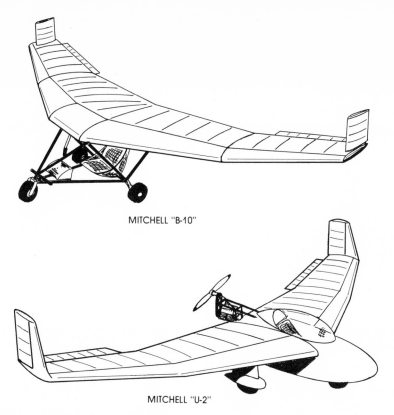

MITCHELL "B-10"

MITCHELL "U-2"

Fig. 12-3. A couple of flying wing ultralights.

Another way to achieve stability in a flying wing is to do what Mitchell did. First of all, select an airfoil with a mild or zero pitching moment for longitudinal stability. For lateral stability, put some dihedral in the outboard wing panels, while adding some sweepback to the center section to aid directional stability. For additional directional stability, attach a vertical fin at each wing tip. To control the wing, add rudders aft the fins, and hang stabilators (Mitchell's secret for stability and control) a small distance below the outboard panel trailing edges.

Prior to Mitchell, flying wing controls had been buried inside the wing profile. Fine at higher speeds, flush controls on a flying wing could be ineffective at ultralight speeds, especially near the stall. Here, stability as well as control could become marginal. Fortunately, the airflow underneath a wing is always attached at positive angles of attack, in addition to possessing energy. The solution was to position the control surfaces beneath the wing. Furthermore, by placing the stabilators at some optimal distance below the lip of the trailing edge, the airflow is actually accelerated over the stabilator, enhancing control effectiveness even more. The stabilators are really small, auxiliary wings that can be rotated simultaneously up for elevator effect, or asymmetrically to function as ailerons. Only up movements of between 2 degrees and 36 degrees are possible, insuring positive pitch throughout the aircraft's operational envelope.

The wing tip rudders provide for both yaw and glide path control. One rudder deflected produces a yaw. Both rudders deflected creates more drag, increasing the angle of descent, providing a good degree of glide path control.

171

In general, flying wings offer a faster pitch response than tailed aircraft due to their low longitudinal damping. In the case of the Mitchell wings, both the B-10 and U-2 models have passed stall and spin tests, as well as wind tunnel tests. The

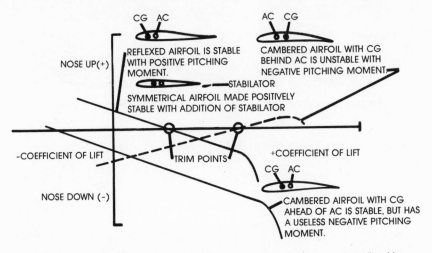

Fig. 12-4. Longitudinal stability of a wing alone varies with camber and the CG-AC relationship.

wings have straightforward stalls, with the nose dropping through like a conventional rear tailed aircraft. Spins are stopped by forward stick and opposite rudder. Turns are lead by rudder, and coordinated with aileron—opposite to conventional configurations.

Section Four
ULTRALIGHT
PERFORMANCE

Chapter Thirteen

A Matter of Balance

An airplane can be flown without the pilot ever really understanding the how's and why's of flight—but it's sort of like playing Russian roulette. If you want to be the safest, most competent pilot you can be, you must intimately know and understand the primary principles of flight.

To begin with, flight, like everything else, is governed by Newton's laws of motion. We were all exposed to them in high school, but a good review is in order to better understand the motions and forces of flight.

All aircraft are subject to four primary forces: lift, drag, thrust and weight—which must be in equilibrium for constant speed, straight and level flight. The lift must equal the weight and the thrust must equal the drag. Newton's first law of motion states it this way: a body tends to remain at rest or in constant speed straight line motion unless acted upon by an outside force. This is actually due to the body's property of inertia. Keep in mind that velocity, by definition, is the combination of speed and direction, and a change in speed or direction will result in an acceleration. Therefore, in an aircraft, an outside force can be developed by either a change in airspeed or a turn. A new balance of forces would have to occur for the aircraft to be in equilibrium once again.

Newton's second law of motion tells us that the acceleration of an aircraft is inversely proportional to its mass and, directly proportional to and in the direction

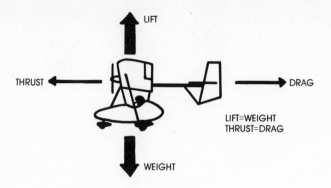

LIFT

THRUST

DRAG

LIFT=WEIGHT
THRUST=DRAG

WEIGHT

Fig. 13-1. The balance of forces in straight and level flight.

of the outside force. In other words, the force is equal to the mass times its acceleration. The simplest example of this is the force of weight—it is equal to the object's mass times the acceleration of gravity. Applied to an aircraft, accelerations and decelerations occur whenever thrust is not equal to drag or, lift is not equal to weight. During a turn, there is an acceleration developed because we are changing direction, even though our airspeed may remain constant. The turn develops centrifugal force, which needs to be balanced by the aircraft banking and pointing its lift vector toward the center of the turn.

Because an ultralight has such a small mass, its inertia is low. Coupled with a low wing loading, this makes it more susceptible to gusts, but it can also be controlled with less force. For the aerodynamically "dirty" designs i.e., those with lots of cable bracing, the low inertia makes itself evident when the nose is pulled-up—the aircraft will lose airspeed quickly because of the large drag forces generated. The large drag force acting on the small mass will cause it to decelerate rapidly.

Newton's third law of motion says that for every action there is an equal and opposite reaction. When an aircraft is resting on the ground, the force of its weight is supported by an equal and opposite reaction from the ground. When in flight, the wing accelerates a mass of air downward and the reaction is upward lift. Also, the propeller accelerates air backward and the airplane reacts by moving forward.

Load Factor

Whenever an aircraft is in straight and level unaccelerated flight, the lift equals the weight and the load factor is one. Whenever an acceleration occurs, such as in a pull-out from a dive or during a turn, the effect is to increase the aircraft's weight or load factor. For example, during a 60-degree bank the load factor is two because the centrifugal acceleration acts on the mass of the aircraft generating centrifugal force. In order for the vertical component of the lift to equal the aircraft's weight, its total lift must be twice as great.

The Four Main Forces of Flight

We can now represent an airplane in unaccelerated, straight and level flight by a system of force vectors. The length of each vector represents the magnitude of the force and the direction of each vector represents the direction of the force. In the figure, point "0" represents the center of gravity; vector "OL" represents the lift;

176

vector "OD" represents the drag; vector "OW" represents the gross weight; and, vector "OT" represents the thrust of the propeller. The airplane is in equilibrium when OT = OD and OL = OW, the simplest case. Before we can describe gliding and climbing flight, it is important to review how vectors are added in a force system.

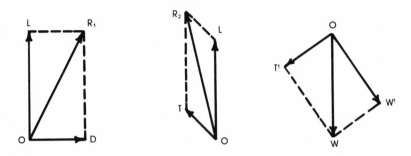

Fig. 13-2. An illustration of the parallelogram law of vectors.

The Parallelogram Law of Vectors

The parallelogram law states basically that any two vectors may be replaced by a third, provided that two form the sides of a parallelogram and the third is the diagonal. Conversely, a single vector may be resolved into two replacement vectors, provided a parallelogram can be formed. Either way, no change will occur in the vector system. In other words, if the system was in equilibrium before the change, it'll be in equilibrium after the change.

Let's suppose we have a vector OR, that we'd like to resolve into horizontal and vertical components. First draw OR, then draw dashed horizontal and vertical lines beginning at point 0. Then draw a dashed horizontal and vertical line from point R.

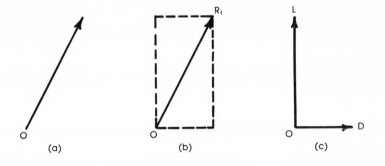

Fig. 13-3. Resolving a force into two perpendicular components.

(NOTE: The horizontal lines must be parallel with each other and the vertical lines must be parallel with each other). You now have a rectangular parallelogram. The lines originating at point 0 are filled in and arrows put on their ends, which are also labeled L for the vertical and D for the horizontal. Now erase the line OR, as well as the R and the other dashed lines and you're left with the horizontal and vertical components of OR, OL and OD.

Another important rule of vectors is that vectors of the same direction can be

177

added head to tail at the balance point of their two origins. For example, if one vector is twice the length of its parallel partner, the balance point between them would be located at a point one-third from the larger vector.

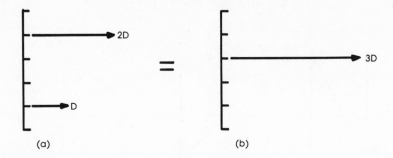

(a)   (b)

Fig. 13-4. Parallel vectors can be added head to tail at their "balance" point.

The Forces In Gliding Flight

If an airplane loses engine power, or is being used as a glider or is making a landing approach with the engine at idle, it is gliding flight. Since there is no longer any thrust being generated by the propeller, an imbalance of forces exist from the straight and level situation, so a new equilibrium will have to be established. The aircraft's nose will lower and the vectors will change. The new flight path will be at some angle below the horizon, and the relative wind will be parallel to this angle.

Since lift, by definition, is perpendicular to the relative wind, the force vector system of the straight and level case is tilted downward to match the glide angle. The lift is no longer equal to the weight. Furthermore, the total vertically upward vector addition of lift and drag which we'll call sustentation, S, is also less than the weight, so the aircraft descends. The weight, of course, remains constant and points straight down. Since our reference axis is now the glide path, we need to

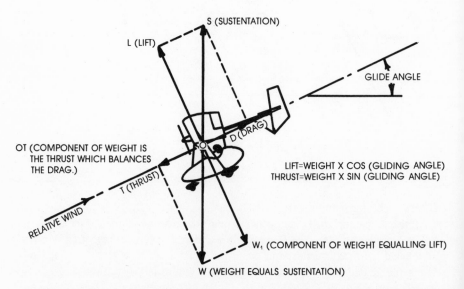

Fig. 13-5. The force balances in gliding flight.

178

resolve the weight vector into components parallel and perpendicular to it. Doing so, we discover that the parallel vector, OT (thrust), is equal to OD (drag) and the (weight), W, is equal to the lift, L, and the system is in equilibrium.

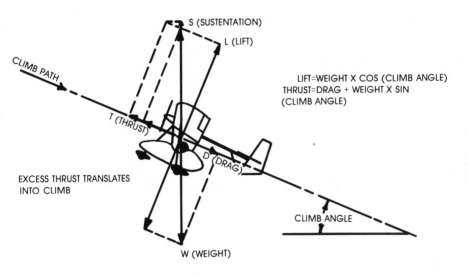

Fig. 13-6. The force balance for climbing flight.

Forces In Climbing Flight

Obviously, no flight is possible without first climbing to some altitude. Climbing after takeoff typically requires full power and also occurs whenever there is more thrust produced than is necessary to balance the airplane's drag at a particular speed. At some speed, generally at 1.4 times the stall speed, the excess power is at a maximum over that required for level flight, resulting in the maximum rate of climb.

In climbing flight, the total sustentation force is made up of the vertical components of the propeller thrust and the wing lift, and it is slightly greater than the weight, resulting in a climb. The weight is then resolved into two components—one parallel to the climb path, opposing the thrust and one perpendicular to the climb path, opposing the lift. It will be seen that the thrust must balance both the aircraft's drag as well as a component of its weight. The excess power required to climb goes directly into lifting the aircraft's weight from one elevation to another, a job which requires more work than propelling the aircraft in straight and level flight.

The most extreme case of a climb would be a vertical climb. In this instance, the thrust would have to equal the weight plus the drag. Needless to say, this would only be possible for a helicopter or a VTOL aircraft such as the Hawker-Siddley Harrier.

Forces In A Dive

If an aircraft is put into a dive or steep glide, the component of the weight parallel to the dive path (OT) is larger, causing the aircraft to accelerate to a speed higher than that possible in level flight. This can be very dangerous and lead to the structural failure of the aircraft. In a vertical dive, the thrust vector, OT, becomes equal to the entire gross weight of the aircraft, resulting in an extremely dangerous situation certainly resulting in structural failure. The aircraft will accelerate to its "terminal velocity," provided it doesn't break when the drag equals the weight.

Chapter Fourteen

Flying Performance

No matter how easily built or how nice the handling qualities of an ultralight may be, it will be a loser with pilots if it doesn't perform well. If it doesn't climb as quickly or cruise as swiftly as the more accepted designs, it just won't be favored by pilots. So what is it that makes an ultralight perform? Let's take a look at this fascinating subject.

Pre-Flight Aspects

For an ultralight to be popular it must be easily constructed in a short period of time. Something that can be done in a week of evenings would fill the bill, and would actually involve a bolt together assembly procedure, rather than an out-and-out homebuilt project.

Transporting an ultralight to the airport or flying field should be as trouble free as possible, and while car-toppability might sound good, it implies time-consuming rigging. A trailerable ultralight with a simple, quick rigging would be the better choice.

Taxiing

Before every flight it is necessary to taxi, or drive the ultralight along the ground. If the pilot has difficulty in doing this he will not be happy, which could be detrimental to the flight he's preparing for.

PROPER TAILDRAGGER TRACKING
REQUIRES RUDDER PEDAL
"DANCE" TO KEEP FROM
GROUNDLOOPING.

ONCE A SIDWAYS MOTION
BEGINS, THE CG MOMENT ARM
INCREASES AND TENDS TO FORCE
THE AIRCRAFT INTO A
GROUNDLOOP.

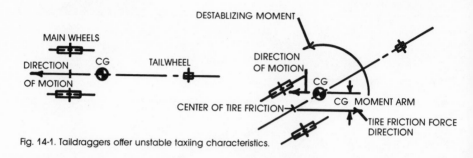

Fig. 14-1. Taildraggers offer unstable taxiing characteristics.

The most important factor in taxi work is the landing gear, and there is no question regarding the superiority of a wide tread tricycle arrangement. The so-called taildragger, i.e., two main wheels in front with a tail wheel, is unstable. With the center of gravity behind the mains, any sideways motion of the airplane will diverge, leading to the tail swinging around to in front of the nose. That's called a ground loop. The tricycle gear, on the other hand, has the center of

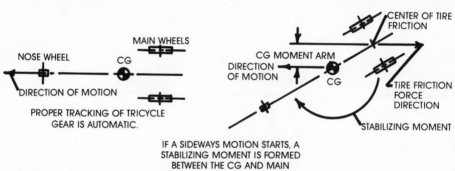

PROPER TRACKING OF TRICYCLE
GEAR IS AUTOMATIC.

IF A SIDEWAYS MOTION STARTS, A
STABILIZING MOMENT IS FORMED
BETWEEN THE CG AND MAIN
WHEELS, FORCING THE AIRCRAFT
TO STRAIGHTEN ITS TRACK.

Fig. 14-2. Tricycle landing gears offer taxiing stability.

gravity properly positioned in front of the main wheels, and makes the aircraft want to straighten itself out.

Another nice aspect of tricycle gear is that it allows the wing to be at a no lift angle while on the ground, a tremendous asset when operating in winds. The wing won't fly until the pilot wants it to, and on landing he can "plant" the nosewheel on the ground, killing the lift to avoid lifting off again.

The Takeoff

The takeoff is the run along the surface during which an aircraft is accelerated from standstill to flying speed. For a pilot to enjoy his takeoff, there is nothing quite like the feeling he gets from a "boot-in-the-tail" acceleration, which comes from a high thrust to weight ratio. The higher performance ultralights can give an acceleration of one-third g or better. An ultralight weighing 450 pounds gross with a static thrust of 150 pounds would produce an initial acceleration of one-third g.

It should be apparent that the higher the thrust and the lower the weight, the greater the initial acceleration. This means we need a reduction drive, with today's high revving two-cycle engines, in order to develop maximum thrust. It also means that the airframe ought to be as light as possible, consistent with structural integrity.

For takeoff acceleration to remain as high as possible during the run, it is important for the aircraft to be clean, i.e., of low drag design. Remember, drag increases as the square of the airspeed, while the thrust diminishes with airspeed.

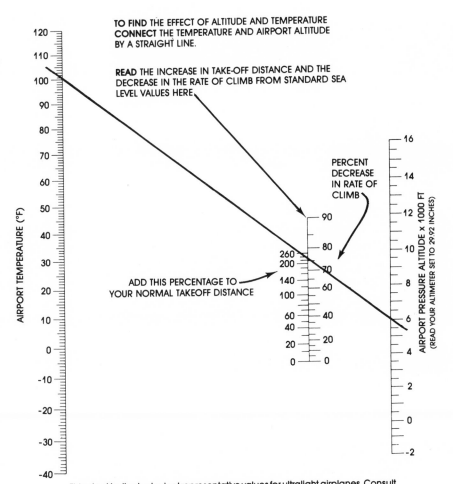

This chart indicates typical representative values for ultralight airplanes. Consult your owner's manual for exact values. Remember that tall grass, sand, mud or deep snow can easily double your takeoff distance.

EXAMPLE: The diagonal line shows that 230% must be added for a temperature of 100° and a pressure altitude of 6,000 feet. Therefore, if your standard sea level takeoff distance, to clear a 50 foot obstacle, requires 500 feet of runway, it would be 1650 feet under the conditions shown. The rate of climb would also be decreased 76%. If your normal sea level rate of climb is 400 feet per minute, it would become 96 feet per minute.

Fig. 14-3. The Koch Chart for altitude and temperature effects.

Besides the airplane design itself, the other item that affects its takeoff performance is the density of the air. As temperature and altitude increase, the air density decreases. In flying, the effects are lumped together in a term called density altitude which directly affects engine power, propeller thrust and takeoff ground speed. The higher the density altitude, the lower the engine power (it drops 2½% per thousand feet), the less thrust the propeller will produce, and the faster the takeoff ground speed required.

As mentioned in the section on aerodynamics, lift depends on the wing deflecting a mass of air in a given period of time—in other words, a mass flow rate. It is the product of density and one-half the velocity squared. Therefore, with increased density altitude, we must go faster for the same lift. Fortunately, airspeed indicators also work on the mass flow rate of air, so the takeoff *indicated* airspeed remains the same for all density altitudes. Nevertheless, we must accelerate to a high *ground speed* in order to takeoff at higher density altitudes. This, coupled with reduced power available from the engine and reduced thrust from the propeller, all adds up to longer distances needed for takeoff.

As an example, suppose your ultralight uses 500 feet of runway to clear a 50 foot obstacle under standard sea level conditions, while climbing at 400 feet per minute. If you were at a pressure altitude of 6,000 feet and a temperature of 100 degrees Fahrenheit, you would need 1650 feet of runway and your rate of climb would be reduced to a sickening 96 feet per minute. If you weren't aware of this and you attempted a takeoff under those conditions in an area the size of which you were used to at sea level, you'd never make it over the trees.

Another factor that affects takeoff distances is the surface condition. A paved runway will provide the quickest, shortest takeoff; anything else requires more. Short grass can add 10% to the run, while tall grass can make acceleration to takeoff impossible. Snow and slush also hinder acceleration, besides potentially jamming or freezing wheels. Snow skis would be your only solution on snow covered fields.

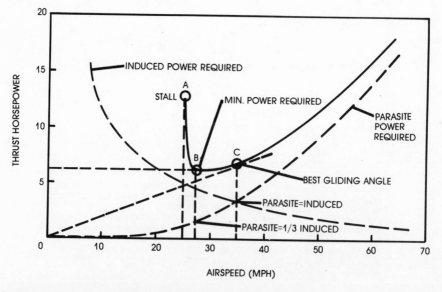

Fig. 14-4. Power required versus airspeed for a typical ultralight at sea level.

The other important field condition is slope. If a grade exists, it is normally better to takeoff downslope and use gravity to assist in your acceleration to flying speed.

Getting Airborne

Once an aircraft is airborne, its level of performance depends on two things— the power required to fly at a given airspeed and the power available at that airspeed. These two items are typically plotted as curves on a graph of thrust horsepower versus airspeed, which can then be used to determine climb, level flight and, descent performance figures. Let's examine a set of these curves for a hypothetical ultralight and discuss their salient points.

Power Required

The power required to fly an ultralight is a function of its drag and how it varies with airspeed—power being the product of drag times velocity. Recalling our previous discussion on drag we know that it is composed of two major components— parasite and induced. Parasite drag predominates at higher airspeeds, while induced drag predominates at lower airspeeds.

At the point of lowest power required, point B, we see that the parasite drag is equal to one-third the induced drag, something that is *always* true. This is also where the sinking rate is at a minimum, meaning the aircraft will remain aloft for the longest period of time while either gliding or under power.

Drawing a straight line from the origin tangent to the curve gives us point C, the speed where the gliding angle is shallowest. Here, we can travel the furtherest distance from a given altitude in a glide, and near maximum range under power. This point is characterized by the fact that the induced drag is equal to the parasite drag—*always*.

Several important relationships are seen to exist between points B and C, and if the manufacturer's figures do not agree with them, somebody's not telling the truth. Be informed that at sea level, the speed for shallowest glide, point C, is

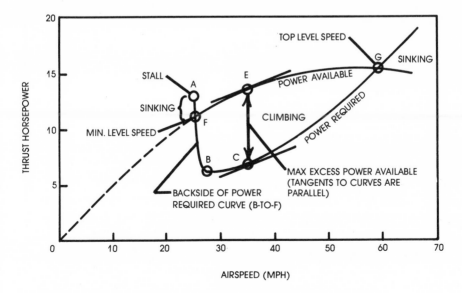

Fig. 14-5. Thrust horsepower required and available for a typical ultralight at sea level.

always 1.316 times the speed of minimum sink, point B. The L/D, or glide ratio, at the minimum sinking speed is *always* 88.6% of the maximum gliding ratio. The sinking speed at maximum L/D is *always* 1.14 times the minimum sinking speed. And finally, the maximum L/D is 101.6 times the ratio of the minimum sinking speed over the minimum sink rate—*always.* Point A is, of course, the stalling speed below which flight is impossible.

Power Required and Power Available

Whereas the power required curve tells us about the aircraft's performance as a glider, plotting the power available curve along with it will tell us about the aircraft's performance under power. The most noticeable thing about the two curves is that they intersect at points F and G. Point F gives us the minimum level flight speed, while point G represents the top level speed attainable by the aircraft. The difference between the two curves from point F to point G is the excess power available for climbing at any given airspeed. The excess power available is a maximum between points C and E and defines the best rate of climb speed. It should be noted that this is where the power required and power available curves have their tangents parallel and is just above best glide speed.

If the pilot desires to fly at speeds other than the intersections of F and G, he must vary the angle of attack accordingly—high angles of attack mean lower speeds and vice versa. If he wishes to maintain a set altitude as well, he must reduce the throttle accordingly. Read that again. These are two of the most important statements regarding aircraft control—*angle of attack controls airspeed while throttle controls climb!* Naturally, less throttle results in less top level speed but, at a given power setting, the stick controls the airpseed, period. Conversely, at a given angle of attack, throttle controls the rate of climb.

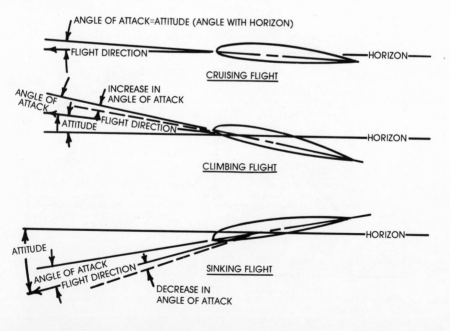

Fig. 14-6. How wing angles vary for different phases of flight.

The Backside of the Power Curve

Increasing airspeed from point B to point G requires greater and greater power, which is what you would expect, just as with any other vehicle. However, *decreasing* airspeed from point B to point F also requires greater power. Yes, contrary to what you may think, it actually requires *more* power to fly below point B. This is the infamous "backside-of-the-power-curve" pilots don't often talk about—an area of reversed commands. It is an unstable area in that it requires constant throttle adjustment to maintain altitude and airspeed. Furthermore, from point F to point A is an area above the power available, meaning the aircraft can only sink to maintain airspeed, no matter if the throttle is wide open! Flying on the backside-of-the-power-curve is dangerous business, first of all because it's so near the stall and second, because it defies our intuitive thinking which equates more power with increased speed. Finally, in order to fly faster than point G, the aircraft must sink, i.e., lose altitude by diving.

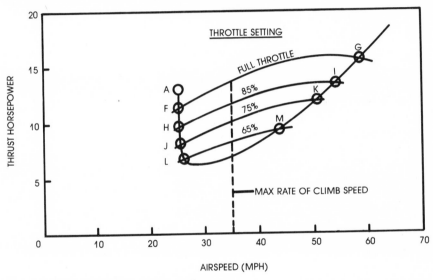

Fig. 14-7. The effects of throttle setting on performance.

Top Speed Versus Throttle Setting

The power available curve presented so far is for wide open throttle. Generally though, the throttle is held wide open only on takeoff and during the climb, in order to minimize wear and tear on the engine. During cruise, the throttle is retarded to anywhere from 50% to 75% of full power. Study of the adjacent figure shows why—very little extra speed is gained in advancing the throttle from say, 75%. The full throttle speed is 59 mph, while the 75% throttle speed is 52 mph—7 mph is hardly worth the strain it puts on the engine. Furthermore, cruising at 65% power produces an airspeed of 44 mph, a good speed for any ultralight, and downright economical, too.

Note: If the throttle is advanced without changing the trim (elevator setting) the aircraft will climb, while maintaining the originally trimmed airspeed.

How Weight Affects Performance

Weight affects the entire performance envelope of an aircraft. Decreasing the

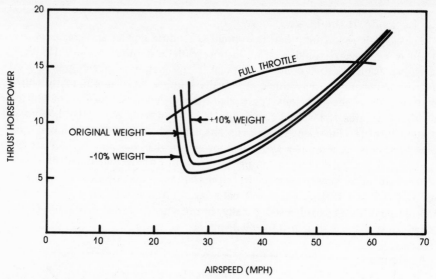

Fig. 14-8. The effect of weight changes on performance.

gross weight by 10% (which means the empty weight on a typical 200 pound ultralight would have to be cut by some 40 pounds) lowers the stall speed from 25 mph to 23.7 mph, while the top level speed increases about one-half mph at full throttle. At lower throttle settings, the cruising speed increases slightly more than that. Lowering the weight by 10% produces an approximate 10% increase in rate of climb however, and is the most important effect of weight on an aircraft.

Increasing gross weight 10% produces detrimental effects on airplane performance. The stall speed goes up from 25 mph to 26.2 mph, the top level speed decreases about half a mph, and the rate of climb decreases about 10%. In other words, the heavier an airplane is, the more power required to propel it at a given airspeed, the affect being most noticeable at the lower speeds.

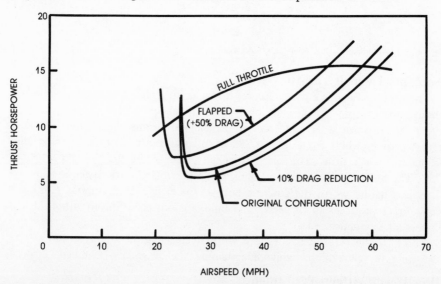

Fig. 14-9. The effect of flaps and drag reduction on performance.

In general, it always pays dividends to keep the weight of an aircraft as low as possible, consistent with structural integrity.

How Drag Affects Performance

Changes in drag have an effect on performance that increases with airspeed. A 10% reduction in drag results in an increase in top level speed from 59 mph to 62 mph. The maximum rate of climb increases about 10%, while the percentage change in climb rate increases still more for the higher speeds. In other words, the power required to fly a given airspeed decreases proportionately with decreases in drag.

The deflection of flaps has a pronounced effect on performance. Flaps not only increase lift, but drag as well. Assuming our wing has an unflapped lift coefficient of 1.5, adding 50% span flaps will raise it to 2.0, lowering the stall speed from 25 mph to 21.65 mph. This also means the landing roll will be reduced, as well. The increased drag of the deflected flaps also increases the sink rate at a given airspeed, which steepens the descent. This is why flaps are so effective as a glide path control.

Flaps can also be used during takeoff, but only at deflections of about 10 to 15 degrees. At these low settings the increased lift is great enough to shorten the takeoff run, while the drag remains relatively unchanged. Flaps on takeoff also have the effect of lowering the best angle of climb speed, which would make it possible to get out of a smaller than normal area.

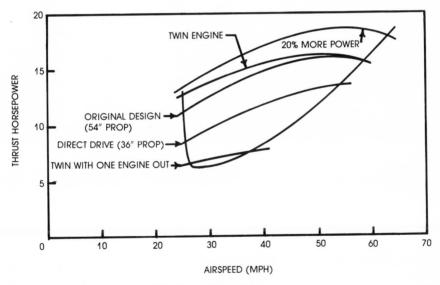

Fig. 14-10. The effects of power and thrust on performance.

The Effects of Power and Thrust on Performance

Everybody knows performance is increased by adding power, but there's more to it than that. Increasing power by 20%, say by adding a tuned pipe, will add dramatically to the climb rate and a little to the top end. The rate of climb will increase approximately 34%, while the top level speed will go from 59 to 63 mph. If a larger, heavier engine is added, however, the changes won't be so great, owing to the increased weight of the engine and its supporting structure. Remember, weight increases lessen performance.

If the original power is divided between two engines, (keeping the propeller dimaters the same as the single), we'll realize a significant increase in performance at the lower speeds. The top end remains unchanged, while the maximum rate of climb increases by about 20% while moving to a lower airspeed. This, of course, says nothing about the increased safety and reliability of a twin. If one engine does quit, our example still has enough power to fly to safety.

Points H, J, and L define the minimum level flight speeds possible at throttle settings of 85%, 75%, and 65%. Notice the higher throttle settings will allow slower speeds. Points I, K, and M define the top level speeds at the same three throttle settings.

The maximum rate of climb, of course, decreases with the lower throttle settings, until it reaches zero at about 50% power. Increasing power from 75% to 100% doubles the rate of climb. In other words, a 33% increase in power produces twice the climb. The best rate of climb speed however, remains unchanged, at about 35 mph for our example.

If we elected to go to a 36 inch diameter direct drive propeller with the same engine, we'd notice a drastic decrease in performance. The climb rate would be cut almost in half, while to level speed will decrease from 59 mph to 55 mph.

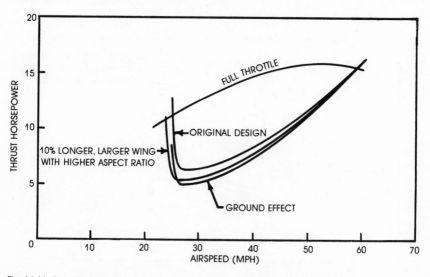

Fig. 14-11. The effect of ground proximity and longer wingspan on performance.

The Effects of Ground Proximity and Wing Span

Pilots will often talk of a tendency to float on landing. This is the so-called "ground effect" in action. A typical ultralight could well have its power requirement lowered by 20% or so, when near the ground. It has the effect of extending the glide and could lead to overshooting a shorter runway. Ground proximity also affects the takeoff. Due to the lowered power requirement, it is possible to takeoff with less power available. The problem arises when the climb takes the aircraft out of ground effect into the realm of increased power requirements, when there is no more power available—as might be the case at a high density altitude condition. A situation like this could lead to an inability to climb over obstructions at the end of the field.

The power requirements of an airplane can also be reduced by increasing the wingspan, area, and aspect ratio. In the accompanying curve, the effect of a 10% larger wing is shown. (We are assuming no increase in weight or drag from the wing addition.) The result is about a 13% increase in rate of climb, due to the greater span and aspect ratio, and a decrease in the stall speed, thanks to the greater wing area. In a rate of climb contest the longer span airplane will always win, all other parameters being equal.

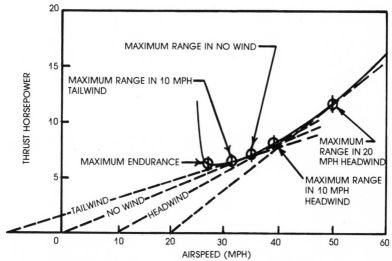

Fig. 14-12. How wind affects the maximum range (L/D) speed of an ultralight.

Cruising In The Wind

The performance figures quoted by manufacturers reflect operations under calm conditions. That's fine, but what happens to cruise performance when the wind blows? Some conventional airplane pilots will tell you that you should increase your airspeed when flying into a headwind, and to decrease it when flying in a tailwind—and that is correct. But how much of an effect does wind have on an ultralight's performance? To find out, we plotted the power required curve and introduced a 10 mph headwind and tailwind.

In calm conditions, the speed for maximum range is slightly above 35 mph—the best L/D speed. As soon as you introduce a headwind however, the situation changes—the best L/D speed increases as well. The headwind effectively moves the origin of the graph to the right, moving the tangent to the power required curve to the right, as well. The new speed to fly for maximum range is then 39 mph, or approximately 10% more than for calm conditions. The ground speed would, of course, be 29 mph. If the headwind increases to 20 mph, the maximum range speed goes up to 50 mph, for a ground speed of 30 mph.

When flying in a tailwind the speed to fly for maximum range decreases. A tailwind has the effect of moving the graph's origin to the left and, therefore, the tangent to the power required curve also moves left. The new maximum range speed to fly is then 32 mph, which is about 10% less than the calm condition maximum range speed. The ground speed then becomes 42 mph.

Crosswind or crabbing flight also suggests that the most efficient cruising speed changes from the calm value. If the crosswind is within 90 degrees of the nose, it will be necessary to increase your cruising speed, depending on the speed of the headwind component. Conversely, if the crosswind is within 90 degrees of the tail, it will be necessary to decrease your cruising speed, depending on the speed of the tailwind component.

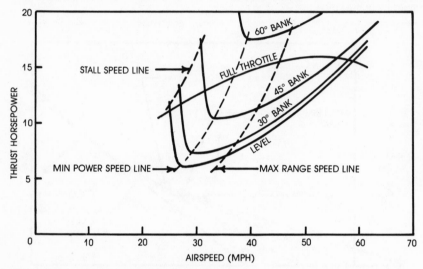

Fig. 14-13. How power required varies with angle of bank.

Turn Performance

By now, we all realize that it takes more power to fly through a turn than it does straight and level. Why? Because as the angle of bank increases, more lift must be generated in order to counteract centrifugal force, while balancing the gross weight. In addition to this, the drag, of course, increases as well and the stalling speed goes up. It all points to an increased power required situation. And, depending on the power available, some maximum bank angle will be obtainable, beyond which the aircraft must lose altitude during the turn.

The figure illustrating "power required versus angle of bank" gives us a good picture of the situation. Below 15% of bank, there is little noticeable increase in power and stall speed. At 30 degrees of bank, the stall speed goes up to about 27 mph, the minimum power required speed increases to 29 mph, while the minimum power required increases about 21%. At a 45 degree bank, the stall speed rises to 31 mph, the minimum power required speed goes to around 33 mph, and the minimum power required increases 41%. At a 60 degree bank, the power required to fly is greater than that available, which implies that the aircraft must lose altitude during the turns.

As the bank angle increases, you will also notice that the speed range becomes narrower—not only does the stall speed go up, but the top level speed comes down. At some bank angle, somewhere around 50 degrees, there's only one speed possible, below and above which the aircraft will sink.

Performance and Altitude

So far, our discussion of performance has been confined to operations at or near sea level under standard atmospheric conditions. As soon as we begin to climb however, things change—the air temperature drops and the density decreases. The thinner air narrows the performance of an aircraft. The power available decreases, while the stall speed increases. The power required increases below the best rate

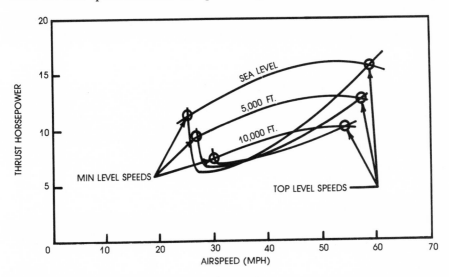

Fig. 14-14. The effect of altitude on full-throttle performance.

of climb speed, and decreases above that speed. The rate of climb decreases, as does the top level speed.

The best rate of climb speed (also best range speed) and best angle of climb speed (also maximum endurance speed) increase with altitude until they equal each other at the aircraft's absolute ceiling (which looks to be about 12,000 feet.) For

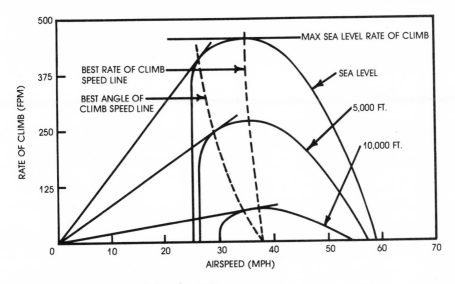

Fig. 14-15. Effect of altitude on climb performance.

193

our example ultralight, the best standard sea level rate of climb is 462 fpm. At 5,000 feet it drops down to around 260 fpm, while 10,000 feet offers a climb rate of only about 75 fpm. The altitude where the climb rate is 100 fpm is considered the "service ceiling," and implies a reasonable amount of excess power available for maneuvering.

We have also plotted a graph depicting how the maximum rate of climb varies with altitude, as well as the time to climb to a given altitude. The maximum rate of climb is inversely proportional to the latitude, between sea level and absolute ceiling. The time to climb is practically directly proportional in the first thousand feet, but increases dramatically with altitude. For our example, it takes a little over two minutes to reach one thousand feet, but it takes ten minutes to reach 4,000 feet, and an hour to reach 10,500 feet.

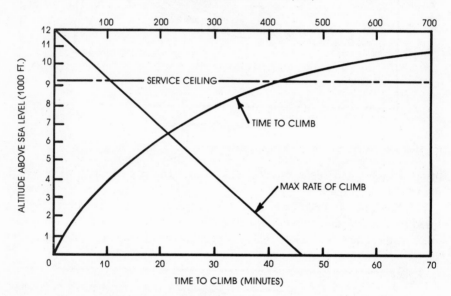

Fig. 14-16. Summary of ultralight climb performance.

Best Rate of Climb, Range, Endurance and Angle of Climb

When the throttle and trim use set to produce an airpseed slightly above the best glide angle speed, which occurs at around 50% for the curves shown, the airplane-engine-propeller combination is most efficient. During a power-off glide, point C gives the most efficient airspeed. But, since propellers are usually designed for cruising speeds, the engine-propeller combination is more efficient at cruise. This means the aircraft under power will have the most excess power available at a speed slightly higher than the best gliding speed. Naturally, the higher the throttle setting, the higher the rate of climb.

Notice that the excess power available doesn't decrease much in a band about 4 mph on either side of maximum, meaning it's not that critical a speed. However, it is better to be on the high side of the "best" speed. It improves engine cooling, and allows for an improved airspeed margin above stall—in case the engine quits.

If we are trying to set a range record, the "best" speed to fly is slightly greater than the best rate of climb speed. If our propeller is designed for climb, the best rate of climb speed might be at or below the best gliding speed. For most practical purposes however, the best rate of climb speed can be used for maximum range and best glide—it all depends on the particular airplane-propeller-engine combination and where it is most efficient.

In order to stay airborne the longest period of time, it is necessary to fly at a speed slightly above the speed for minimum sink. Power-off, minimum sinking speed will yield the longest time aloft for a given altitude. Power on, the engine propeller efficiencies cause an upward shift in this speed. Slightly above maximum duration speed, an airplane will attain its steepest angle of climb, again depending on the engine-propeller combination.

Chapter Fifteen

Operational Performance

All aircraft are designed to provide a particular level of performance. Ultralights, as a group, are designed specifically for economical recreational flying for distances of under 100 miles from home base. Cross country transportation is simply not their purpose in life. They are flown primarily for the sake of flying, and the joy and relaxation it provides.

In designing an ultralight, several parameters must be considered for each phase of flight, as well as for pre-flight tasks. To determine the most important parameters in a design, we can assign value points to each of: construction time, rigging time, transportability, ground handling, stability, engine control responsiveness, reduction drive, power, low speed controlability, wing area, aspect ratio, drag, glide path controls, and low weight.

The author has tabulated the various operational phases of pre-flight and flight performance, and tried to develop some priorities for each parameter under a given phase. Each parameter is given a number from one to ten, ten being the best, in an effort to identify the most important.

Pre-Flight Aspects

Low rigging time is essential for minimum pilot frustration. This implies minimal loose parts and less chance for damage and simple "wearing-out" of the airframe, from so much assembly and disassembly. It is rated at 10 points. Low construction time is important too, for recreational pilots are interested in flying, not building. It is second to rigging, so it rates a 9.

An ultralight is a flying machine first, and a ground transportable item last. Portability should not design an airplane; thus, if a trailer is required we'll credit 8 points. If the design is car-toppable, which implies a high rigging time, it receives a 7 for this parameter. An ultralight that can not be transported at all, meaning it must be kept at an airport or field, is not to be considered. A low empty weight is also desirable from a man-handling point of view, and is good for 6 points.

Takeoff

Takeoff requires that an aircraft must first be easy to handle on the ground, and the best landing gear arrangement for that is the tricycle. Taildragger landing gear may be nostalgic, but they're not stable—they have a tendency to ground loop, i.e., for the tail to swing around in front of the nose. Easy ground handling rates a 10.

When first lifting off the ground the airspeed is low, requiring low speed control effectiveness. We must be able to handle crosswinds and some gustiness to continue with a safe, controlled takeoff run. Low speed control rates a 9.

A high static thrust is desirable next, for a short ground run. The object is to build up speed as quickly as possible to get off the ground. High static thrust implies a reduction drive with today's high revving two cycles, and deserves an 8.

A low empty weight will also contribute to a shorter takeoff—there's simply less mass to accelerate to flying speed—it gets a 7. A large wing area will also contribute to reduced flying speed and a shorter takeoff run, but it requires more structure and creates more drag. We'll give it a 6.

Climb

The climb to altitude should be done as quickly as possible, which requires a static thrust and therefore a reduction drive. The climb should also be done as quietly as possible, another good reason for the large diameter propeller possible with a reduction drive, and we'll call it a 10.

Another way to improve climb is to reduce the empty weight. The less weight the airplane has to lift, the faster it'll climb to a safe altitude. Low weight deserves a 9. Lowering the drag will also enhance the climb. This calls for a large wing area and a high aspect ratio in order to reduce the coefficient of lift required and hence lower the induced drag. We'll give aspect ratio an 8, and large wing area a 7.

If a climb is to be made safely, the aircraft must be stable and possess minimal adverse yaw. Good stability minimizes pilot anxiousness to get to altitude, while minimal adverse yaw minimizes trim drag, enhancing the climb. A stable airplane rates a 6 during climb. To climb as quickly as possible requires a low drag design, which rates 5 points.

Cruise

The primary requirement during cruising flight is that the airplane be stable. This reduces pilot workload and makes flying a pleasant experience. Stability at cruise gets a 10.

A reduction drive is nice during cruise because it provides an abundance of excess thrust and climb power, coupled with a quiet propeller. The pilot is comforted knowing he can climb in a downdraft and doesn't have to worry about going deaf. A reduction drive is worth a 9 during cruise.

It is well for an ultralight to be a low drag design for cruising efficiency (low fuel consumption) and the ability to regain speed quickly from a nose-up attitude caused by a gust or whatever. Low drag deserves an 8 during cruise.

A high aspect ratio is beneficial to airplane efficiency and lowered fuel consumption and is good for a 7. Low weight deserves attention as well for the less weight there is to carry, the less fuel the airplane burns. Let's give it a 6.

Descent and Approach

The descent and approach phase of flight requires the airplane to be stable and possessed of minimum adverse yaw. The pilot wants the aircraft to transition smoothly from cruise, and to execute an accurate pattern and final approach. He needs stability to minimize his workload as he concentrates on the field. A stable airplane rates a 10 during descent and approach.

If an engine stoppage occurs during cruising flight, and you are required to land in a field the size of a "postage stamp," you may find it necessary to descend at a steep angle. In other words, you need glide path control. This can be provided by flaps, spoilers or tip draggers. All will increase the airplane's drag and steepen the glide path. Glide path control deserves a 9.

A most desirable situation during the descent and approach is one where, once the throttle is retarded never to have to advance it until on the ground for taxi. It should certainly be a goal for all pilots to develop this technique, but it isn't always possible. A sudden gust could interfere or a crosswind may blow you from your intended pattern. The throttle is the only answer, and it must be responsive to the pilot's wishes, and so deserves an 8.

Landing

Just as during takeoff, and aircraft must possess good low speed control with minimal adverse yaw while landing. A wing must be able to be picked up "right now," and the nose lowered if a sudden gust causes problems just above the ground. Low speed control warrants a 10 during landing.

Once on the ground, an airplane must be easy to handle. This means a tricycle landing gear is desired and it rates a 9.

Along with good low speed control, the engine must be responsive for the same reasons as, it might be needed to abort the landing and "go around" the pattern for another try. Good engine response gets an 8.

To make the landing as easy as possible, an airplane must be stable. The airplane should be able to correct for gusts with minimal help from the pilot. Stability rates a 7 during landing.

Glide path control devices rate a 6, since they could also be useful during landing. Flaps can, of course, be used to lower the landing speed and hence the roll out. Spoilers or tip draggers, if normally held on during the approach, can be released just before landing if some additional distance needs to be covered before touchdown.

Low weight should also be mentioned, since it lowers the landing speed. It deserves a 5.

High Density Altitude Flight

Not everyone lives and flys his ultralight at the standard conditions of sea level and 59 degrees F. Flight under high density altitude conditions puts extra demands on an aircraft that must be considered.

The most noticeable effect of high density altitudes is a decrease in the engine's power at the rate of about 2½% per thousand feet. This lowers the rate of climb and lengthens the time required to climb to a selected altitude. It means that we need more power for higher density altitudes in order to maintain performance. High performance rates a 10.

Next on the list would be a reduction drive for maximum thrust. High power without a way to transfer it into the air efficiently is a waste. Reduction drives deserve a 9.

Once we have enough thrust horsepower to fly, we need the airplane to be stable, as in cruising flight at lower density altitudes. Stability rates an 8.

A large wing area and high aspect ratio are necessary to reduce the coefficient of lift and therefore the induced drag. High aspect ratio rates a 7, while high wing area gets a 6.

Next on the list is low speed control response with minimum adverse yaw. High density altitudes mean the air is thin, and controls tend to get sluggish. Low speed control rates a 5.

Low weight will also help the cause here, and rates a 4. And finally, low drag is important for descent performance and rates a 3.

Ranking of Ultralight Aircraft Design Parameters

If we go through the above analysis of the various design parameters in each operational phase, we arrive at their relative importance to ultralight aircraft design. Adding them all up results in the following ranking:

1.	Stability	41
2.	Reduction drive	36
3.	Low weight	32
4.	Aspect ratio	29
5.	Low speed controllability	21
6.	Easy ground handling	19
7.	Engine responsiveness	16
8.	Low drag	16
9.	Glide path controls	15
10.	Wing area	12
11.	Power	10
12.	Rigging time	10
13.	Construction time	9
14.	Trailerable	8
15.	Car-toppable	7

The above parameter ranking is, of course, the author's opinion, but designers and pilots should consider them in their analysis and selection of an ultralight.

Flying Performance and Design

As stated at least once before, the design of an airplane is loaded with compromises—a gain in one area for a loss in another. In designing the optimum airplane, the goal should always be to have the gross weight as low as possible while meeting all the operational requirements. For an ultralight, we want a docile and forgiving airplane that handles well, climbs well, and is inexpensive to own and operate. This "formula" calls for a low wing loading, low power loading and high thrust consistent with takeoff, climb, cruise, and altitude performance.

As evidenced by the previous discussion, ultralight designers should strive for low weight, long wings, and low drag. Lack of concern in these areas will yield an inferior performing aircraft. Weight affects the entire performance spectrum and should always be given top priority in design. Low weight can be facilitated by sound engineering design and proper use of materials. Use of a light weight engine pays untold dividends in that the airframe weight will also be reduced. A gain in weight results in an ever increasing spiral for the heavier an airframe gets, the heavier it needs to be in order to support the extra weight, and so forth. Weight in an ultralight has noticeable affects on rate of climb and stall speed. Range is also affected by changes in weight. All weight reductions must, of course, make no concessions to structural integrity.

Since ultralights are low powered and slow flying, attention must be paid to their wingspan. Rate of climb is one of the most important aspects of ultralight performance and, in order to achieve a good climb a large span is necessary (remember, large wingspans minimize induced drag at low speeds.) Large spans also facilitate low cruising speeds and long range.

Ultralight designers also need to pay attention to parasite drag. Some say drag is unimportant at ultralight speeds, and while that may be true at 30 mph, it isn't true above that. Besides, more drag means a larger engine and more weight, so it is always important to minimize drag. Dumping more power into an airplane is easy, but shows a lack of engineering expertise. However, installed power is important when it comes to high density altitude operation, which will probably decide the engine selection. In general, we should strive for an ultralight that does its job with as little power as possible.

Bibliography for Ultralight Flight

(1) Abbot, Ira H. and Albert E. Von Doenhoff, "Theory of Wing Sections", Dover Publications, N.Y. N.Y.

(2) Batchelor, B.K., "An introduction To Fluid Dynamics", Cambridge University Press, Cambridge, England.

(3) Bisplinghoff, R. L., Holt Ashley and Robert L. Halfman, "Aeroelasticity", Addison-Wesley Publishing Co., Inc., Reading, MA.

(4) Chanute, Octave, "Progress In Flying Machines", Lorenz and Herweg, Long Beach, CA.

(5) Crawford, Donald R., "A Practical Guide to Airplane Performance and Design", Crawford Aviation, Torrance, CA.

(6) Crouch, Tom D., "A Dream of Wings — Americans and the Airplane, 1875-1905", W. W. Norton and Co., N.Y., N.Y.

(7) Duke, Neville and Edward Lanchberry, "The Saga of Flight", Avon Books, N.Y., N.Y.

(8) Etkin, Bernard, "Dynamics of Flight", John Wiley and Sons, Inc., N.Y., N.Y.

(9) Harper, Harry, "The Evolution of the Flying Machine", David McKay Co., Philadelphia, PA.

(10) Gene Husting, Herring historian, L.I., N.Y.

(11) Jarrett, Philip, RAes. Pilcher historian, London.

(12) Lanchberry, Edward, "A.V. Roe", The Bodley Head, London.

(13) Markowski, Michael A., "Ultralight Aircraft", Ultralight Publications, Hummelstown, PA.

(14) McCormick, Barnes, W., Jr., "Aerodynamics, Aeronautics, and Flight Mechanics", John Wiley and Sons, N.Y., N.Y.

(15) McFarland, Marvin W., "The Papers of Wilbur and Orville Wright", McGraw-Hill Book Co., Inc., N.Y., N.Y.

(16) Means, James, "The Aeronautical Annual" (1895, 1896, 1897), W. B. Clarke and Co., Boston, MA.

(17) Perkins, C.D. and Robert E. Hage, "Airplane Performance, Stability and Control", John Wiley and Sons, Inc., N.Y., N.Y.

(18) Pope, Francis and Arthur S. Otis, "Elements of Aeronautics", World Book Co., Inc., N.Y., N.Y.

(19) Pritchard, J.L., "Sir George Cayley", Parrish, London.

(20) Roughley, T.C., "The Aeronautical Work of Lawrence Hargrave", Americana Archives Publishing, Topsfield, MA.

(21) Thurston, David B., "Design for Flying", McGraw-Hill, N.Y., N.Y.

(22) Von Mises, Richard, "Theory of Flight", Dover Publications, N.Y., N.Y.

(23) Hoerner, Dr. S.F., "Fluid Dynamic Drag", Midland Park, NJ.

(24) Hoerner, Dr. S.F., "Fluid Dynamic Lift", Midland Park, NJ.

202

The Ultralight Library
Practical Aviation Books From Ultralight Publications

ULTRALIGHT AIRCRAFT - The Basic Handbook of Ultralight Aviation (Revised 2nd Edition) by Michael A. Markowski. This is the best selling (over 25,000 sold), definitive word on ultralight flying and aircraft. Divided into four sections, it covers: **Ultralight Aircraft Described**, including – Specifications to over 40 Aircraft • Performance • Handling • Drawings • Pilot Reports • **The Basic Ultralight Flight Manual** describes the specialties of ultralight flying – Principles • Stability and Trim • Low Speed Flight Control Techniques • Stalls • Spins • Landing • Traffic Pattern • Slideslipping • Crosswinds • Crabbing • Instruments • Density Altitude • The Koch Chart • Wind Chill Factors • Navigation • Flight Planning • Winds and Weather • **Ultralight Propulsion** includes – Engine Operation • Trouble-Shooting • Engine Reviews • Propellers • **Appendicies** cover – Test and Study Guide • FARs • Manufacturers and Dealers Lists • Plus much, much more. Ultralight Aircraft is highly recommended and endorsed by industry leaders. "Every aspect of ultralight aviation is covered by a professional who knows!" 320 pgs., 220ill., 6x9 in.
Order No. 1 .... **Paper $14.95** .... **Hardbound $21.95**

ULTRALIGHT AIRMANSHIP - Intermediate To Advanced Flying Skills, by Jack Lambie. What can you do after you've learned the basics of ultralight flight? What's next? This exciting new book spells it out in clear, concise language — how you should fly to make use of, avoid, and operate in various atmospheric conditions, with specific advice and flight descriptions by experienced flyers. Large weather systems and circulation patterns, as well as the intricacies of micrometeorology (airflows around valley passes, mountains, behind trees, buildings and other obstructions) are described in detail. Learn how to handle turbulence and fly practically anytime you want to — you don't have to limit yourself to just mornings and evenings. If you know what's in this book! ULTRALIGHT AIRMANSHIP is your ticket to total mastery of the air — your "roadmap-to-the-sky." 144 pgs., 110 ill., 6x9 in.
Order No. 2 .... **Paper $9.95** ..... **Hardbound $17.95**

ULTRALIGHT PROPULSION - The Basic Handbook of Ultralight Engines, Drives and Propellers, by Glenn Brinks. If you expect to fly with utmost confidence, you must know your power system — its characteristics, and idiosyncracies — inside out. The two-cycle ultralight engine is a stranger to most pilots, but it must be thoroughly understood before flying can be done with any degree of safety. ULTRALIGHT PROPULSION describes the incredibly important details of power — how it is produced and transmitted into the air to provide performance — from a pilot's point of view. The book describes ignition systems, carburetors, starters and starting, spark plugs and how-to read them, exhaust systems, break-in and trouble-shooting, teardown, inspection and reassembly, modification, accessories and controls. The various drive methods are reviewed — belts, gears and direct. The practical aspects of propeller operation, care, balancing, tracking and safety are presented. ULTRALIGHT PROPULSION tells you what power is all about — from a drop of gasoline to a rate of climb. It tells you how to get maximum performance, reliability and life from your power system. It's your most important *"tool"* for a good running engine. 224 pgs., 110 ill., 6x9 in.
Order No. 4 .... **Paper $13.95** ..... **Hardbound $20.95**

THE ULTRALIGHT LOG BOOKS

Designed with the ultralight pilot in mind, each has space for over 500 flight entries. Each is bound in a beautiful, colorful, heavy leatherette cover for long wearing durability. Fits in hip pocket! These log books are the only way for you to keep track of your valuable flight experience, aircraft usage, and engine operation. Know your proficiency level as well as your ultralight's condition.

THE ULTRALIGHT PILOT FLIGHT LOG, includes: Pre-flight inspection procedures, load factor and stall speed vs bank angle chart, ultralight traffic pattern, density altitude/Koch chart, landing factors and field perspectives, wind chill chart, and the flying-speed-of-an-ultralight.
Order No. P-1 .... **$3.95**
THE ULTRALIGHT ENGINE LOG, includes: Trouble-shooting guide.
Order No. E-1 .... **$3.95**
THE ULTRALIGHT AIRCRAFT LOG
Order No. A-1 .... **$3.95**
ULTRALIGHT CROSS-COUNTRY PLANNING AND LOG SHEETS (50 forms)
Order No. C-1 .... **$1.59**
BUMPER STICKER: FLY AN ULTRALIGHT AIRCRAFT – DISCOVER A NEW DIMENSION IN FLIGHT (3"x12": Yellow & Black on White)
Order No. BS-1 .... **$1.59**
T-SHIRT (Same wording as bumper sticker, S, M, L, XL – four color)
Order No. TS-1 .... **$9.95**

— ——

TO ORDER: Put your name and address on a sheet of paper. List the book title and order number, and include cash, check or money order to cover book cost plus $2.95 for postage and handling of total order. **Send to: Ultralight Publications, P.O. Box 234, Dept. UP, Hummelstown, PA 17036 USA.**